MARKETING ON A TIGHT BUDGET

BUDGET

An Action Guide to Low Cost Business Growth

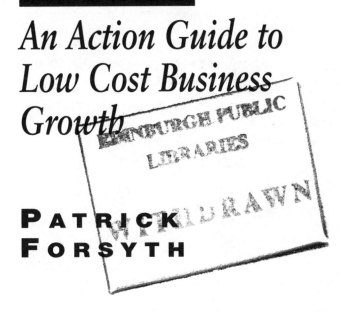

PATRICK FORSYTH

KOGAN
PAGE

Other titles by Patrick Forsyth, published by Kogan Page:

30 Minutes Before a Presentation
101 Ways to Increase Your Sales
Everything You Need to Know About Marketing
How to Be Better at Writing Reports and Proposals
How to Motivate People
Marketing Professional Services

First published 2000

Kogan Page Limited   Kogan Page US
120 Pentonville Road   163 Central Ave, Suite 2
London N1 9JN   Dover NH 03820
UK   USA

British Library Cataloguing in Publication Data

A CIP record for this book is available from the British Library.

ISBN 0 7494 3263 2

Typeset by JS Typesetting, Wellingborough, Northamptonshire
Printed and bound in Great Britain by Clays Ltd, St Ives plc

Contents

Preface   ix
Acknowledgements   xi

1. A Blueprint for Success   1
Competitive pressures   4
The groundwork   5
Who is the customer?   7
Market research   8
How you approach the market   11
Overseas markets   12
The promotion mix   14
Promotion costs   17
The 'one hour marketing plan'   21
Summary   22

2. Telling the World   24
The buying process   25
Public relations   27
Advertising   35

3. Promotion by Post   49
What makes direct mail successful?   50
The elements of the mail shot   55
Measuring results   67
Cost and timing   69
A creative approach   69
Large and small-scale promotions – examples   77

4. Sales Promotion   86
Categories of promotion   87

The creative factor 90
Promotion methodology 97

5. Making an Exhibition of Yourself **100**
Dangers and opportunities 102
Preparation 103
What must you do once you've decided to take a stand? 103
Making your presence persuasive 105
Establishing contact 107
After the ball is over 109

6. Face-to-face Persuasion **112**
Low cost prospecting 114
Techniques to make your approach persuasive 118
Using product information effectively 122
Using the benefit approach 127
Asking the right questions 129
The service element 131
Customer development 132

7. On Your Feet **135**
What might go wrong? 138
The planning stage 139
What will be presented? 148
Tell 'em, tell 'em and tell 'em 152
Rehearsal 154
Attention to detail 154
Beware overkill 156
Action after the event 158
A worthwhile method? 160

8. Selling at a Distance **164**
Prospecting 165
Keeping in touch 176
Regular order – taking calls 177

9. Creating Sales Without Leaving Your Desk **185**
Getting it right 187
Customer service 191
But... 196

10. Systems to Assist Sales   **201**
Enquiries   202
Customer records   204
Customer development   206
Complaints   208
Debtors   210
Customer opportunity analysis   211
Dotting the 'I's   215

11. The One Hour Marketing Plan   **216**
The business plan   217
The promotional plan   228

Afterword   238
References   240
Index   241

Preface

*Just about the time you think you can make
ends meet, somebody moves the ends.*
PANSY PENNER

Those who manage a small business are regarded by many people
as being in an enviable position. Often their own boss, they are
independent, able to be flexible, to concentrate on the things that
interest them, to organize matters their way and generally get on
with the job in hand. By contrast, larger enterprises may seem slow,
bureaucratic, committee driven and steeped in rhetoric. The reality
is often all too different.

Under pressure, the manager of the small business often seems
besieged by a plethora of difficulties that conspire to make running
the business unnecessarily complicated. Paperwork, administration,
VAT, legislation, the bank and more paperwork, administration...
you see the problem. Furthermore, a business – any business –
ultimately stands or falls by its success in the market place. It needs
sufficient customers buying its products and services often enough
to produce both the necessary financial return and the wherewithal
to invest and secure future growth.

Now the manager doubtless recognizes this, but the process of
ensuring it happens can still prove problematic for a variety of
reasons. The manager may be a specialist. Perhaps the business was
founded on engineering or design skill and it is this at which it is
best, but the business-generating process is less its real forte. And as
that process may seem complex and is certainly time-consuming,
this too may contribute to it being neglected. Besides, business-
generating activities cost money, real money, paid out in advance
with no guarantee that they will bring in results that will repay and
exceed the money spent. However, somehow new business must be
brought in.

This book takes a practical look at just how it can be done with some likelihood of success (though there are not, regrettably, any guarantees) and in a way that minimizes both the cost and the time involved. It is designed to act as an *aide-mémoire* and a stimulus to action.

The first chapter sets the scene, laying out how marketing can act to bring in the business. It also demystifies the terms, for instance showing clearly the difference between marketing and selling. It then presents a practical view of marketing planning. This shows how to keep the process manageable and provides precise, succinct guidelines that really help in running the business. Ten further chapters follow, so that the total provides a 10-point action plan, which systematically explores the mix of options from which action may be chosen to provide a flow of business. The final chapter, The One Hour Marketing Plan, enables you to pull the ideas together and plan ahead, for the short and longer term.

Each chapter reviews the role of its particular area and shows how the techniques involved can act to make it effective. The topics are chosen not to review the whole of marketing activity equally, but to focus particularly on those activities that make up the 'best buy' mix of activities for those in smaller companies trying to get the greatest impact from a tight budget. In each case the coverage is designed first to help ensure marketing techniques are used appropriately and effectively (there being no better way to fritter away a budget than to use it on ill-chosen or poorly executed activity). Secondly, it is designed to illustrate low budget ideas and examples to help bridge the gap between reading about something and implementing it. There is intended to be a logical progression throughout, but each chapter is also designed to make sense in its own right, so that the book lends itself to being 'dipped into' to investigate particular topics of interest.

Overall, its intention is clear: to explain the need for promotional and sales activity to bring in the business, to demonstrate which methods allow this to be done on a low cost basis, and to set out how this can be used to secure and build the enterprise into a larger and more profitable small business.

Patrick Forsyth
Touchstone Training & Consultancy
28 Saltcote Maltings
Heybridge, Maldon
Essex CM9 4QP
Spring 2000

Acknowledgements

Although I run a small business, like to think I do so successfully and certainly know the problems of so doing, this alone does not qualify me to write a book on marketing on a tight budget. In doing so I have drawn on more than 20 years experience in marketing consultancy and training, most recently with my own firm. My work has regularly involved me with small businesses (as well as large) and from such involvements and the people I have met through them, I have learnt a great deal.

So, I am grateful to all those I have met along the way and who, wittingly or unwittingly, have helped my experience to grow and whose ideas, thoughts – even chance remarks – have helped put me in a position to write this text. For some years before starting my own firm I worked with the Marketing Improvements Group, and it was during this time and with their encouragement that I wrote my first books. Some of these, for example *Making Marketing Work* (written with Gerard Earls and now out of print) acted as antecedents for this volume and I gladly acknowledge how everything about my association with them has assisted my later writing. Others who have assisted specifically with particular parts of this text are mentioned in context throughout the text.

This book is directed at small and medium-sized businesses, but it draws just a little on another volume published by Kogan Page: that is, my book *Marketing Professional Services* (which is a handbook directed at firms providing specialized professional services such as accountancy).

Also due a mention are Jacqui Forsyth, who continues to support, advise and demonstrate that her formal knowledge of English is much more great (sic) than mine, and Judy Chick who provided invaluable – and seemingly wondrously accurate – help with typing the first draft. Also my partner Sue, whose head I bite off much too often for interrupting my chain of thought when I have a writing project on the go, but who is simply invaluable in so many ways (now please will you spare a moment and send the invoice to the publisher?).

1

A Blueprint for Success

Planning a sound foundation for bringing in the business

The only place where success comes before work is in the dictionary.
VIDAL SASSOON

Running a small/medium-sized business was never easy. In recent years competitive pressures and, in many markets, recession have combined to make it downright difficult. If the business you manage is your own, you know also that it is vulnerable, as good as its last month's sales – and there is a great deal hanging on its success. Such a feeling is only marginally reduced if you manage the business for someone else or share the risk.

So, how do you make sure of your success? There is, regrettably, no magic formula and it is not the intention of this book to suggest otherwise. Success depends on a number of things, such as what you sell, where and how it is sold, and the quality of every kind of service involved before, during or after the sale is made. All are important. So too are the processes of 'bringing in the business', many of which are usually encompassed by the word 'marketing'.

The promotional techniques that form part of marketing are what this book is primarily about.

There are no magic formulae among the promotional techniques either. Success is not a question of selecting one technique and coming up with some wonderfully creative interpretation of that – one exceptionally persuasive advertisement perhaps – and everything else looks after itself. There are guiding principles that help, however, and ideas that can make a practical difference. This book sets out to review at least some of these. Success cannot be guaranteed, but we can certainly work at increasing its chances in a practical way. Before turning to the individual techniques, there are a number of other issues concerned with the overall process, or those important to the setting up of the business, which must be addressed. Such aspects are at least as important to success as the clever promotional ideas (though you will need some of those too). So, while this is *not* intended in any sense as a theoretical marketing textbook, some scene setting is necessary and, as we will see, is included only for practical reasons. It is to these overall issues which we now turn and, if they lead to a need for detail which is not covered in the remainder of the text, this is noted.

We will start with the issue of marketing. It is a confusing term and can conjure up images of such things as mass advertising which are inappropriate or beyond the scope of the small business. Marketing is, in any case, much more than a euphemism for advertising or selling. It can be a confusing term because it has a number of different connotations. Three are important to us here:

1. Marketing is a *concept*. The marketing concept suggests that any business will do better if it is customer-oriented. This means, specifically, that if customer needs are identified, recognized and satisfied – giving people the product or services they want and delivering it in the way they want it – we are likely to do better than by trying to sell what we have or think is right. This is, of course, no more than common sense. However, many businesses fail or do less well than they might because of a shortfall in customer orientation. Think about that shop of which you said, despairing at their lack of service, 'I will *never* go in there again', to verify this for yourself.
2. Marketing is a *function*. This means someone has to 'wear the marketing hat'. Someone is – must be – responsible for doing things in the marketing area, and not only doing them, but

initiating and coordinating them also. In a small company this sometimes concentrates the mind. While wearing the marketing hat does not necessarily mean that person does everything, if resources are limited it may mean he or she does most things, and for the owner/manager there may be no one else – thus who is responsible for marketing is a one-choice question, at least in the short term.

3. Marketing is an umbrella term for a *variety of techniques* that are used within the function. These include some mentioned only in passing here (though none the less important for that), such as pricing, forecasting or sales management, and others, namely the promotional and sales techniques with which this book is predominantly concerned. It is here that confusion regarding the word 'marketing' is most apparent. Marketing is not, as we have seen, limited to advertising. Nor is it any other kind of promotional technique in isolation. It is not selling either, though this is important and consists specifically of all forms of person-to-person *persuasive* communication. All such factors are component parts, techniques under the umbrella of overall marketing activity. Here the emphasis is on what can be best used to bring in the business and what mix of activities best suits smaller firms on a tight budget. As such we will investigate a variety of promotional techniques, and also various manifestations of selling, including telephone contact and sales systems, which make sure that what is done is truly effective and thus gives the best result for the money it costs.

This begins to put marketing in perspective. However, there are other important issues to consider before simply starting to deploy any promotional or sales techniques. The first of these is the market itself, the stage on which your business must perform. No business operates in a vacuum, cut off from outside influences, and marketing must be done while recognizing many influences – some positive, others less so. A whole range of influences are involved:

- *Economic:* financial factors can seem restrictive and they often are. Think of borrowing rates, taxes, operating costs, etc.
- *Technological:* these may be positive or negative, for example technological development may assist (as word-processors have assisted the quality of written presentation) but often necessitate investment and training.

- *Social:* changes here again may have a variety of effects, as with the demographics of the ageing population in the UK and elsewhere, which may provide opportunities (retirement homes/ holidays) or reduce the potential in other sectors.
- *Political:* government may affect markets also, with legislation on anything from the compulsory testing of pharmaceutical products to safety measures concerning car tyres, and other areas, for instance the prevailing or future level of spending on schools or roads.

In recent years another influence has been added to this list:

- *Environmental:* the green movement has affected many product areas, with advertising featuring recycled paper (toilet tissue/ stationery) or the omission of harmful chemicals or additives (CFCs have now largely disappeared from aerosol products).

COMPETITIVE PRESSURES

The market – the world of customers and potential customers – is essentially dynamic. Change is the norm. Customers are fickle, their loyalty hard won and easily lost. And always competition is in evidence, often all too active. Competition is something that must always be borne in mind; all promotion activity is received by the market alongside a cacophony of other messages – many, for the smaller business, louder than those that it can put out. And what exactly is competition? This may seem an obvious question. If you make pens or undertake printing, then your competitors are surely other pen manufacturers and printers. Yes; but competition is broader than this. Consider the pen manufacturer who makes, let's suppose, medium-priced ballpoint pens. His competitors make similar pens. But what about fountain pens, roller balls and fibre tips? And pencils? These are competitors too, as are dictating machines and typewriters and, of course, writing instruments of all prices from throwaway to solid gold. Still further factors must be included. Many pens are given as presents, so competition includes alternative present choices, a book, a music CD, a necktie and so on. Many more are given as business gifts, so competition here ranges from pen pots to calendars. I could go on. You can consider in a similar way any product or service you may provide; it may be a sobering thought.

Despite this there is a widespread belief that a good product will sell itself – the old idea of the 'better mousetrap', which crops up in a quote that is well worth bearing in mind:

> They say if you build a better mousetrap than your neighbour, people are going to come running. They are like Hell! It's marketing that makes the difference.
>
> Ed Johnson

Though to some extent a good product will sell, for most the moral is *actively* to bring in the business.

The realities of competition and the need to bring in the business do not make doing so any easier. In a small business there often seems to be more than enough to do just running – perhaps 'administering' is a better word – the business, without the need to spend valuable time searching for customers. But, make no mistake, marketing and, as we shall see, the promotional aspects of it, takes time. Success goes, in part, to those who recognize this, invest the necessary time and do so (equally important) at the right moments to maintain the continuity of the business. So, and I make no apology for saying it at this stage, success *does not just happen.* Think of the old saying that the trouble with opportunities is that they so often come disguised as hard work (something I have no difficulty recalling as I write the first chapter of a book of almost 250 pages!). While time is money, investing it more wisely than your competitors can perhaps qualify as a low cost tactic.

Next we turn to planning and, before you reject it and turn to Chapter 2, admit that planning is necessary. We will consider here the minimum necessary and do so primarily with the 'one hour marketing plan', for surely no business is really so small that you can say that you cannot spare an hour?

THE GROUNDWORK

Every business must have a good product. However, it's worth saying a little more about the nature of the 'product' – a word that encompasses a number of different things.

Whatever you offer to the market, applying a marketing approach will increase its chances of being successful. Yet there is no magic formula, certainly no one, single way to proceed or to apply marketing principles that is right for every product. In any case, not all 'products' are products; some people sell services. The differences here are important.

Products

Products are tangible. The customer can see them, touch them and, depending on what they are, sit on them, use them, or take them to bits and put them together again.

Every product will, by its nature, involve particular factors connected to its physical characteristics. A car can be taken for a test drive, a fax machine can be demonstrated, a pen can be written with – in other words some sort of trial is possible. And these aspects can be used in the way the marketing of them is approached. For example, if customers demand a demonstration or test, then the supplier must make that opportunity readily available. How many people would buy a pair of shoes if they couldn't try them on, for instance? As we will see, the physical product is not the only thing that is important, for every product has its own image, and the prestige or status that goes with it may be critical; this is an additional aspect to cultivate and use.

Services

Services, on the other hand, are intangible. Customers cannot touch them and, most important of all, cannot test them in advance. Whether they are getting a suit dry-cleaned or hiring an accountant, they simply do not know until they commit to using them (and incur costs) whether they will like the result. Although this is inherent to the nature of services, customers *do not* like it. Before they buy they look for anything that will provide evidence of the likely outcome and indicate the quality, or lack of it, to come. This means that the peripheral issues become disproportionately important. If a shop, for instance, does not look right to some customers they will not go in, perhaps fearing it is 'cheap' in the low quality sense. Conversely, if an accountant's office appears too plush, potential clients may conclude that it will be very expensive and go elsewhere. Here the other major factor is the people, and services are often referred to as 'people businesses' for just this reason. The people must sell themselves before they can sell their service and the whole approach must cultivate a level of credibility that gets over the problem of the service being untestable.

WHO IS THE CUSTOMER?

In either case, another major difference exists in terms of to whom the product or service is sold. Some items are sold direct to the end consumer or user, while others are sold to people who resell them. Take a simple item like a pen. This may be sold to a retailer who sells it on to its customer, or sold (in quantity) to a company that wants to give them away to their customers as a Christmas gift, or an offer linked to the sale of its own product. Other items are only bought to be included in the marketing of another organization, like containers to pack products in (what is called derived demand) or to use in running their business – everything from stationery to computers. So the differences here are considerable.

In reading on, you should therefore bear in mind that ultimately what makes marketing work is how it is adopted and implemented to suit the unique characteristics of any business and its customers. There are general principles, of course, but marketing is a creative process made to work not by slavishly following exactly what others do, but by adapting ideas to suit the individual circumstances of a particular business. In the text that follows, examples are intentionally taken from a variety of different product and service areas in a number of industries. Even so, you should try to relate everything to your own – no doubt unique – business as you go. Some ideas will perhaps suit without any change, while others will prompt thoughts and help you towards the best way forward for your own company.

Whether you provide a product or service, and assuming it is good, it does not have to be unique (there are very few of those) but it does have to be sound. Whatever level it is at in the market – remember the pen example earlier, with a product range running from inexpensive throwaway to very expensive gold – it must be based on customer need. And the place to establish that, the only place in fact, is in the market.

MARKET RESEARCH

Market research can provide an objective, external view of the company's product. It can help answer questions like these:

- What product do people want?
- What service do they want with it?
- What is the right technical specification?
- How should it be sold?

Now I'm not advocating that every business venture commence with a costly investment in formal market research (and it can be costly). Some products certainly succeed without this, some becoming worldwide successes. The Sony Walkman, surely a success by any standards, is a prime and much quoted example (though sitting next to someone on a train who is at full volume and does not share your taste in music may colour your view of this). It is proof also that hunches can pay off, indeed many would suggest that hunches are an important creative element in marketing. The point is that most usually it is one element; hunch alone may lead to disaster. If hunch becomes personal conviction – obsession even – this is more likely. Sir Clive Sinclair, very successful with a series of electronic and computer products, failed completely with his electric car project, and the C5, nicknamed the electric bath chair, passed rapidly into history.

So, while formal market research may not be essential, a genuinely objective eye on the customer certainly is. This may mean no more than an ear to the ground, more usefully a number of other ears to the ground – people who will give you a genuine view and not tell you what you want to hear. You may usefully put together a network of such people. Beyond that, market research may well be useful and, while it is outside the scope of this book to itemize all the techniques, some short comments may help. There is more to research than the person with the clipboard who stops you in the street. Not only is market research an area with its own techniques and technicalities, it also has to relate to overall marketing activity, particularly in planning and decision making. This definition of market research and brief discussion of its purposes is taken from *The Effective Use of Market Research*, by Robin Birn.

The traditional definition of market research is:

> The systematic problem analysis, model-building and fact-finding for the purpose of improved decision-making and control in the marketing of goods and services.

The two basic purposes of research are:

1. to reduce uncertainty when plans are being made, whether these relate to the marketing operation as a whole or to individual components of the marketing mix such as advertising or sales promotion;
2. to monitor performance after the plans have been put into operation. In fact, the monitoring role has two specific functions: it helps to control the execution of the company's operational plan and it makes a substantial contribution to long-term strategic planning.

Thus it is implied that research is not some academic information tool, but a means of providing guidance to help management take the appropriate action more certainly and with less risk. This may involve the setting of overall strategy, or details such as whether the product should be red or blue; the latter is typical of factors that seem minor, but can have a marked effect on the level of success of the product.

Another view propounded by Robin Birn in the same book is what he calls the 'win–win' aspect of market research. To quote him again:

> Using research is a 'win–win' situation for those who interpret it and action it effectively. Management 'wins' first time when the research confirms its prejudices, ideas and experiences, so providing reassurances that it is taking the right decisions. It 'wins' a second time if the research provides new information or gives a new focus or emphasis on the subject being researched.
>
> Over a period of time users of research also find that they 'win' a third time. If they take a step back to look at the original findings of the research objectively then they can design more interesting and more relevant research than had been completed originally. Research therefore helps management to 'win' by indicating the action it needs to take.

This, too, confirms that market research must not be other than a practical and cost-effective contribution to marketing success. Consider what it can do and the various kinds of research that are involved:

- *Market research:* this focuses on the market and the customers, and can produce information about who (what kinds of people) buy and what quantity might be sold.
- *Product research:* highlights what is felt to be right and wrong with the products (or services) technically, operationally or in other ways.
- *Marketing method research:* this can produce useful comment on how the company communicates with customers, showing whether it is regarded as clear, appropriate and whether it happens often enough to maintain recall.
- *Motivational research:* aims to show *why* people buy a product or use a service and what they feel about it.
- *Attitude surveys:* show the image a company has and how that affects people's likelihood of purchase.

Research is expensive and can be sold 'by the yard', that is researchers are sometimes reluctant to undertake anything except work of some substance, so it needs approaching with care. However, omitting it can be even more expensive if action is being taken without information from the market that would change what is being done and increase the chances of success.

It is, in fact, very easy to get so close to the business that you feel you know the answers: what people think of the company or what it provides. Yet you may be, in reality, lacking the real view. Or, worse, you may be focusing on what you would *like* to be the view rather than what actually is the case.

At the very least you should keep a genuinely objective eye on your customers and listen to what they say. They may volunteer some information, but you may want to take action to prompt some regular feedback. This need not be expensive and examples of this sort of simple, low-cost feedback-gathering include:

- the questionnaire you find in hotel bedrooms and on restaurant tables;
- the assessment form given out at the end of a seminar;
- the reply card accompanying direct mail letters or sales letters;

■ the form inside the box in which a product is packed;
■ follow-up telephone calls after a product has been sold and should be in use;
■ feedback forms at the end of a period of doing business (such as an accountant may send out at the end of the year);
■ interactive, information-collecting procedures on Web sites.

All of these cost little to organize and can give you some regular feedback over a period. Consider, too, the people in your company who have the most customer contact, including sales or service staff and whoever handles any complaints you may get, as the consensus of their views may well be worth canvassing regularly. No single information source is infallible; but the use of a number of such feedback mechanisms will build up a useful picture. Beyond this, major moves, a new product or significant change may need more research – and more expenditure. If so, so be it, but check out carefully any research you plan to do and whom you involve in it (ask the UK Market Research Society, which operates a strict code of practice and can recommend researchers who are members). You could access a researcher with experience of and interest in the smaller company.

Above all, *listen* to the feedback you get from any such activity, by all means merging findings with your (objective) judgement, considering the implications and, if necessary, acting accordingly. Ultimately, success only comes from offering what the market wants, so never be so sure you know that you close your mind to all other evidence.

HOW YOU APPROACH THE MARKET

Remember that *how* you sell your product or service is as important as *what* you sell. There are many alternatives:

■ *direct to the customer* –
  – door to door;
  – mail order;
  – catalogues;
  – sales people;

■ *via 'middlemen'* –
  – retailers;
  – wholesalers;
  – agents and distributors.

The most obvious (or what most direct competitors do) may not be best for you. Even within the same product group there may be many options. Take books, by way of example. Traditionally they are sold through bookshops; perhaps that is where you bought this one. But direct mail is used extensively, especially for business books, as are book clubs. One publisher of children's books uses 'party plan' marketing, selling to mothers of small children at gatherings organized on the basis of the better-known Tupperware promotional parties. And books were an early player in the burgeoning world of e-commerce, pioneered by Amazon.com. Any method chosen must make sense to customers and you must make it work for you.

Another point to consider here is that distribution method is variable. It is not, as is sometimes thought, fixed. Just because your industry or company has operated with a particular form of distribution for many years, it doesn't mean this will always be the case. The method may become outdated. For example, some flights are sold through 'bucket shops' (discount-oriented retailers) and now from Web sites, rather than through conventional travel agents – who once felt secure in their monopoly. Or a new method may be radically different. Books being sold through direct mail rather than conventional retailers is certainly different, and while often the customer pays more (for postage), it's convenient and it works.

In other instances change may be made specifically to win new business rather than to continue existing business on a different basis. The children's book 'parties' mentioned earlier were introduced for just this reason and are designed to communicate with customers who might never go into a bookshop. As the payment of the 'party organizers' is largely on commission, the costs – at least the fixed costs – are less than those of other methods simply being extended.

OVERSEAS MARKETS

For the small company, export markets may seem to need a prohibitive investment and hardly to be a low cost way of bringing in the business. Again, the full details of export marketing are beyond our brief here, yet consider: there may be certain factors that not only make it worth looking at, but cost-effective too.

First, there is a good deal of assistance available from banks, Chambers of Commerce and, in the UK, from the Department of Trade and Industry. Ask them about grants for research, exhibitions, about trade missions, and simply about the information they can give. All this can contribute tangibly to creating success.

Secondly, there may be particular factors that make overseas markets attractive. Marginal costing is often applied to export sales. In other words, the fixed costs of producing a product are paid for by local sales and anything extra, sold in overseas markets, that produces any contribution over and above the variable costs (eg materials) is regarded as profitable.

These two points may be worth bearing in mind and may produce opportunities for some firms, but remember, if there is anything particular about your offering (or experience or contacts – perhaps you speak a second language) this may assist, though neither will reduce the time and effort of getting export business started.

Perhaps my business can provide an example of the special factors that make overseas markets attractive. Part of my work done in training is giving 'public seminars', promoted for attendance by people from a variety of companies. As preparing these takes time and needs research, this is costly if the seminar runs only once. However, if it can be offered in different locations (regionally perhaps) and – with some adaptations – overseas, this amortizes the preparation costs and produces additional profit opportunities. It is always worth checking through the various aspects of any business to see if something applies and can be used practically.

For the smaller company, personal motivation about where you might enjoy travelling to can come into it – why not, if it's your company? However, this must coincide with genuine opportunities. If it does, and if this has been checked and you are sure of this coincidence, then travel can enliven any business. This is how part of this book was written by the swimming pool at one of the best resorts in Malaysia, when working for an international hotel group! I am, in this context, at least according to government categorization, an 'invisible' export, because I market a service. Overseas sales can also, in some instances, be achieved without even travelling overseas, for example by using intermediaries such as agents or distributors.

But we must now return to mainstream business and set out an overview of the promotional elements that are a key part of both the process of marketing and its planning.

THE PROMOTION MIX

This phrase describes a number of techniques and implies a plethora of combinations and ways of using them. Figure 1.1 shows how different communications methodologies act in different ways in respect of the customer, from those having influence at a distance and being directed at large numbers of people, through to selling that is one-to-one. A brief comment about each of the ingredients of the communications mix will serve to put them into context at this stage.

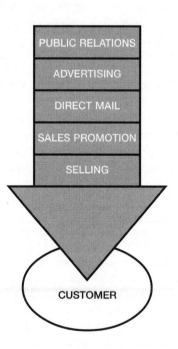

Figure 1.1 The mix of persuasive communications

Public relations

The aim of public relations is to create or maintain a favourable climate of opinion in which the company can operate. Every company will have an image; the question is whether it projects the right image and how strongly. It is therefore important that the actual image reflects what is wanted.

The first task is to define those 'publics' among whom the company wants to have a favourable reputation. Having identified the target groups, the next step is to find out what image these groups currently have of us:

- Do they know the company and its product/service?
- What is their perception of both?

Some information can be obtained by keeping your ear to the ground. If this isn't sufficient, more formal market research may have to be undertaken.

Once the present awareness and image have been identified, PR targets can be set, ie who should know and perceive what about the firm? We can then decide which PR promotional techniques will be most cost-effective in achieving the desired image goals. Typical methods include the following:

- *Press publicity and developing good relationships with writers and editors.* This does not just happen, it means taking the initiative, following up and delivering – sticking to deadlines and so on (for example, tell your local radio station who would be prepared to comment where appropriate).
- *Membership of influential bodies.* This does not just happen, either. Someone (the right person) actually has to belong and take part. It takes time, but can lead to good contacts. Bodies such as trade associations in industries where you work or want to work should not be neglected. Contacts, once obtained, should be followed up systematically; this may be as simple as arranging to ring them rather than waiting for a call that never comes.
- *Use of 'house style' for brochures and written material.* Again, this does not just happen: someone has to decide what is needed and has to maintain the image. Brochures are a case in point: many are the same as everyone else's, out of date, introspective, boring and – at worst – banal. A vital point to remember is that

it is not just a case of making them look better (though this is important); getting the message right comes first and a graphic designer may not be the best person to do this. This may be better done by working with a copywriter or consultant, though you cannot escape the responsibility of deciding *what* is said.

■ *Public-speaking engagements.* These have to be sought out and you have to field the right person, ie someone who can make a presentation of a quality that will get them asked back (not whoever is most senior or happens to be available). If done well, presentations can certainly produce enquiries.

Advertising

Advertising can be defined as communication in bought space, the intention being to attract existing and potential customers. It can:

■ provide information;
■ attempt to persuade;
■ create dissatisfaction with competitive offerings; and
■ reinforce existing purchasing habits.

Limited budgets may preclude mass action here, although some activity may be important. Therefore, while advertising may be used beneficially, especially by larger organizations, the 'best buy' in terms of promotional mix for the medium-sized firm will perhaps be public relations and promotion, planned and followed through as well as reactive, coupled with an increasingly planned, organized and professional sales effort.

Direct mail

Direct mail, or promotion through post, is another matter. Essentially only a specialist form of advertising, it has considerable relevance for some and warrants its own chapter (see Chapter 3).

Sales promotion

Sales promotion encompasses a number of elements, often used together as a 'campaign' around one particular product/service or at one time. Newsletters, events, briefings, etc are good examples, though any business must select what is appropriate and, of course, work only with what is acceptable to and effective with its customers.

Selling

Selling must be planned and deployed in a way that increases the chances of business resulting from it. For some it is an area of weakness. Promotional activity is often geared primarily to producing enquiries rather than what happens when an enquiry is received. Someone is referred to you, perhaps by an intermediary, and telephones your business. What happens? Is the response specifically designed to give the best impression? Who speaks to the enquirer? Who goes to visit them if appropriate? Is the response to the enquiry designed to increase the chances of business resulting, or is the call dealt with by whoever is in the office that day, has time or is most senior?

To ensure success, responsibilities, even targets, must be set for individuals. Sales activity must then be deployed so that the techniques are made full use of, but customers remain content. This way you run the kind of customer contact you want and that customers find they like.

It is the totality of this mix that will bring in the business, and subsequent chapters focus on all the main elements in more detail.

PROMOTION COSTS

One vexed question regarding promotion relates to cost. How much should you spend on it? The exact sum of money will, of course, be different for every business, but here are some guidelines for deciding the budget.

Percentage of sales

To take a fixed percentage based usually on forecast sales relies on the questionable assumption that there is always a *direct* relationship between promotional expenditure and sales.

It assumes, for example, that if increased sales of 10 per cent are forecast, a 10 per cent increase in promotional effort will also be required. This may or may not be realistic and depends on many external factors. The most traditional and easiest approach, it is probably the least effective.

Competitive parity approach

This involves spending the same amount as the competition, or maintaining a proportional expenditure of total industry appropri- ation or an identical percentage of gross sales revenue compared with competitive firms. The assumption is that in this way market share will be maintained. But competition may be aiming at a slightly different sector, and including competition in the broadest sense is no help. If we can form a view of competitive/industry activity it may be useful, but the danger of this approach is that competitors' spending represents the 'collective wisdom' of the industry and the blind may be leading the blind!

It is important to remember that competitive expenditure cannot be more than an *indication* of the budget that should be established. In terms of strategy, it is entirely possible that expenditure should be considerably greater than that of a competitor – to drive them out – or, perhaps for other reasons, a lot less.

Remember that no two companies pursue identical objectives from an identical base line of resources, market standing, etc, and that it is fallacious to assume that all competitors will spend equal or proportional amounts of money with exactly the same level of efficiency.

What can we afford?

This method appears to be based on the premise that if spending some- thing is right, but we cannot objectively decide the optimum amount, whatever money is available will do. Many companies look at:

- what is available after all the other costs have been accounted for, ie premises, staff, selling expenses;
- the cash situation in the business as a whole;
- the revenue forecast.

Then advertising and sales promotion are left to share out the tail-end of the budget. In these companies, more expenditure is considered to be analogous with lower profits; in others, more expenditure on advertising leads to more sales at marginal cost, which in turn leads to higher overall profits.

Fixed sum per sales unit

This is similar to the percentage-of-sales approach, except that a specific amount per unit (eg per holiday sold) is used, rather than a percentage of pound sales value. In this way, money for promotional purposes is not affected by changes in price. This takes an enlightened view that advertising expenditure is an *investment*, not merely a cost.

What have we learnt from previous years?

The best predictor for next year's budget is this year's.

Are results as we predicted? What relationship has our spending to the competition? What is happening in the market? What effect is it having and what effect is it likely to have in future? We can do the following:

- *Experiment* in a controlled area to see whether we are under or over spending. As the chairman of Unilever once said: 'I know that 50 per cent of our advertising expenditure is wasted, the trouble is I don't know what 50 per cent.'
- *Monitor results*. This is relatively easy and the results of experiments with different budget levels can then be used in planning what to do next (though we must always bear in mind that all other things do *not* remain equal).

Task method approach

Recognizing the weaknesses in other approaches, a more comprehensive four-step procedure is possible. Emphasis here is on the tasks involved in the process of constructing a promotional strategy. The four steps of this method are:

1. *Analysis*. Make an analysis of the marketing situation to uncover the factual basis for the promotional approach. Marketing opportunities and specific marketing targets for strategic development should also be identified.
2. *Determine objectives*. From the analysis, set clear short- and long-term promotional objectives for continuity and 'build up' of advertising impact and effect.
3. *Identify the promotional tasks*. Determine the promotional activities required to achieve the marketing and promotional objectives.
4. *'Cost out' the promotional tasks*. What is the likely cost of each element in the communications mix and the cost-effectiveness of each element?

What media are likely to be chosen and what is the target (number of advertisements, point of sale material, sales promotions, direct mail leaflets, etc)? For example, in advertising, the media schedule can easily be converted into an advertising budget by adding space or time costs to the cost of preparing advertising material. The sales promotional budget is usually determined by costing out the expenses of preparing and distributing sales promotion material, etc.

The great advantage of this budgetary approach compared with others is that it is comprehensive, *systematic* and likely to be more *realistic*. However, other methods can still be used to provide 'ball park' estimates, although such methods can produce disparate answers, such as:

1. we can afford £10,000;
2. the task requires £15,000;
3. to match the competition we need £17,500;
4. last year's spending was £8,500.

The decision then becomes a matter of judgement, allowing for our overall philosophy and objectives.

There is no wholly accurate mathematical or automatic method of determining the promotional budget. The task method does provide, if not the easiest, probably the most accurate method of determining your promotional budget.

More details about each of the promotional techniques shown in Figure 1.1 and touched on here appear in the subsequent chapters. However, with this broad view and particularly with the relationship between the different techniques in mind – they are not simply alternatives – we can now review planning. Indeed, the existence of a plan, or rather the working out of one, should be regarded as the first key to success.

THE 'ONE HOUR MARKETING PLAN'

Many businesses – and not just smaller ones – have no real plan. Many have only a budget, which at least gives them a figure to aim at in terms of sales and profit and a way of estimating, monitoring and controlling costs. A few have neither plan nor budget, like the business manager who told me his objective was to make 'as much money as possible'; whether in a good or bad year this is no more than a self-fulfilling prophecy. As such it is not very helpful in any practical sense.

The only rationale for a marketing plan is that it is *helpful*; that it provides practical assistance in the process of running – of directing – the business. If it does that, surely it's worth an hour or so. You can buy voluminous texts on marketing planning (and don't let me put you off reading one, if you need and want more detail), but the purpose here is the reverse.

The one hour marketing plan (see Chapter 11) sets out the basics, the minimum needed to create a useful plan, and presents a set of formats for doing just that. The text leads you sequentially through the thinking that is necessary for your business, and the formats have been limited to seven (and a calendar). It is not, I believe, unmanageable and (not counting reading this section) an hour spent thinking it through and making notes can be very worthwhile. Maybe you can be persuaded to spend more time than this, but certainly even this basic exercise is useful. It is up to you whether the notes are written up and typed to create a more formal plan, but there are reasons to do so: more of this later.

Bear in mind that the plan should *not* be restrictive, since it aims to provide a route map, not a straitjacket. Specifically, the marketing plan has three main aims:

1. To be certain that all the objectives set by the firm are clearly related to specific actions (and by corollary that large amounts

of expensive time are not taken up by activities that have little or no effect on the achievement of objectives).

2. That the individual efforts of all staff are concentrated on the actions specified. In particular, all staff should be aware of the key priority actions which keep the firm in business today and tomorrow. At its simplest, this could be ensuring that every account is examined to identify additional business potential or perhaps that invoices are submitted immediately they are due.

3. That all the activities specified in the plan can be measured, assessed and improved as the planned year progresses (realistically, some fine-tuning is likely).

In order to separate the plan from the flow of this text, some guidelines to the planning process generally and the promotional planning side in particular appear in Chapter 11. It is an important area and a planned approach is highly likely to be more cost-effective than an *ad hoc* approach. Before turning to Chapter 11 you may like to read Chapter 2 and beyond to persuade yourself that there is a sufficient range of activities involved to need planning. The fact is, you ignore planning at your peril.

Chapters 2 to 10 investigate individual areas. They follow a logical progression, broadly from the more general – advertising that addresses potential customers in some quantity – to the more individual, including selling. Some chapters link together. For instance, the one on telephone selling follows those on selling and presentations and does not repeat the basic principles involved. Otherwise, the remainder of the text lends itself to being 'dipped into' and does not necessarily have to be read sequentially.

SUMMARY

This chapter has reviewed a good deal of ground in comparatively little space, but its message provides an important basis for the remaining chapters.

Any organization aiming to 'bring in the business' efficiently and cost-effectively must *plan* to do so. It is important to:

■ understand something of marketing and be aware of its implications;

- recognize the restrictions inherent in running the business as you want;
- keep a continuous eye on both the customer and competition;
- have a sound (preferably researched) basis for believing your product/service can succeed;
- take a broad view of opportunities (such as how you can relate to your chosen market and where in the world business opportunities lie);
- view and use the mix of promotional techniques in a selective rather than *ad hoc* manner; and
- create a thought-through and realistic plan that sets out not simply *what* you want to achieve, but *how* it will be done, and particularly how promotion and sales will act to bring in the desired type and volume of business in a way that is timely and profitable.

None of this need be prohibitively time-consuming and, however difficult it may be to fit in thinking time, it can be made very worthwhile. Without it business is swept along by events, a formula that will hardly recommend itself to anyone and which can result in business being lost by default.

2

Telling the World

Public relations and advertising

The meek shall inherit the earth, but they will never increase market share.
WILLIAM MCGOWAN

Few businesses are perceived as being unique. Few are without competitors; indeed the world in which most businesses operate seems to have got more and more competitive in recent years. However excellent your product or service may be, the world is unlikely to beat a path to your door uninvited. Most accept that some form of promotion is necessary and see the apocryphal businessman who did not believe in promotion, until he had to put a 'For Sale' notice outside his premises, as a real warning.

Successful promotion is rarely *ad hoc* and the point about it needing to be planned and co-ordinated was made in Chapter 1. This chapter is concerned not only with how promotion – particularly public relations and advertising – works, but also with individual ideas. But whatever ideas you have and implement, they will do better as part of a planned, integrated approach.

Whatever you do, whatever technique you use, each activity must play its part in initiating, increasing and maintaining awareness of what you offer to your customers. The intent is to move customers from a total lack of awareness through to the point at which they actually buy. And, hopefully, buy again. Overall, the intention is to change attitudes and ultimately the aim is to change from non-usage of a product to usage or repeated usage.

THE BUYING PROCESS

The stages in the buying process are:

- unawareness;
- awareness;
- interest;
- evaluation;
- trial;
- usage;
- repeat usage.

Each stage represents a tangible change and is worth examining sequentially.

Unawareness – awareness

This is the stage during which a potential buyer moves from no knowledge of a product or situation towards a position where they know about it. The buyer's attitude is nearly passive, with a major need to be informed. Promotion is targeted at:

- telling the buyer that your product exists;
- creating an automatic association between the needs and the product.

Awareness – interest

This is a movement from a passive stage to an active stage of attention. The buyers will have their curiosity aroused by the product's newness, appearance or concept. The buyers' response, however, can be conscious or subconscious. Promotional objectives are:

- to gain the buyer's attention through the 'message';
- to create interest (motivation);
- to provide a succinct summary of the product (information).

Interest – evaluation

Buyers will consider first the effect of the product on their personal motivations (lifestyle, image, practical needs, etc) and will then look at the effect on external factors. They will pass through a process of reasoning, analysing the arguments and looking for advantages. Depending upon their needs, they might look for improved efficiency or economy, uniqueness, reassurances or safety. Through promotion, you attempt to:

- create a situation that encourages the buyer to start this phase of reasoning;
- discover the buyer's relevant needs;
- segment and target buyers according to the 'needs' requirements.

Evaluation – trial

This is a key movement from a mental state of evaluation to a positive action: that of trial. The buyer's basic requirement is for a suitable opportunity to use the product. Promotional objectives are to:

- clearly identify usage opportunities;
- suggest usage when these opportunities occur.

Trial – usage

The buyer will take this step if the trial has been successful. The objectives of your promotion are to:

- provide reminders of key elements, such as brand, advantages, etc;
- emphasize the success and satisfaction;

■ remind the buyer of usage opportunities and provide supporting proof via third-party references.

Usage – repeat usage

This is the final objective of promotion. When buyers move from occasional usage to constant usage, they will be in a state where selection of your product is (virtually) automatic – at least for the moment. Your objectives are now simpler:

■ to maintain the climate that has led to satisfaction;
■ to maintain an acceptable image;
■ to keep confirming the key qualities of the product.

Both public relations and advertising may have a role to play in this overall process and we will now review them in turn.

PUBLIC RELATIONS

PR plays an important role in cultivating an image and can also take a form which prompts greater change in the potential customer's attitude, perhaps even prompting enquiry or, better still, purchase. Some of the things that come under the heading PR may seem obvious, but all are important and the effect is cumulative, with seemingly small things contributing to what ultimately becomes a noticeable positive effect.

This is certainly an area, for the most part, of low cost approaches and though it is, of course, possible to spend tens of thousands of pounds using PR consultants, much can be done more simply. This does not mean spoiling the ship for a ha'p'orth of tar and it may be worth spending just a little more than the minimum in some of the basic areas to achieve what you want. Here are some examples:

■ *Business cards*. These are important and must look right. Consider both the information on them (should they have a description of what your business does, a picture or a map of where you are?) and the production (should they be in two, or even four, colours, embossed, or have a shape cut out of them?)

Some elements can achieve both impact and information – a picture, map or quotation.

■ *Letterheads.* Similar factors apply here as to cards, though the overall design (of both) should be modern, professional and uncluttered. Don't put *everything* on the letterhead, though a description of the business, or an endorsement or quasi-recommendation such as membership of a professional body may help.

■ *Name badges.* These are used by some businesses – banks, travel agents, restaurants – and help personalize service and create the confidence of dealing with someone identified.

■ *Business name.* Choose carefully, since you may be stuck with it for a long time. Consider how descriptive it should be, also how memorable. Something too clever, or unpronounceable, may be self-defeating. In businesses where the name appears on the premises, it should be well presented, whether on a shop front, a brass plate by the door of an office or whatever.

You may well be able to think of simple, low cost approaches, items that make a point and say something about a company and, best of all, are seen as appropriate or useful. For example, one company whose customers travel some distance to find them offers a cassette tape of recorded directions to play in the car.

Every company has an image. The question is only what *sort* of image is projected. The kinds of factors that help to build and maintain image are:

■ a well, and promptly, answered telephone;
■ an easy-to-remember telephone number (ending in, say, 1234 or 4444);
■ clear communications – a letter to confirm an appointment, explain location and acknowledge an arrangement – all help;
■ regular contact, showing you care.

Note: some things are best avoided because they make you *appear* small, for example having only a mobile telephone number.

Press relations

All the things mentioned so far you do yourself, but another important part of public relations is *press relations*; this is where you recruit others – particularly the media – to help you put over a message. This needs some organizing, almost certainly some persistence and there is no guarantee it will work as you want it to. It is, however, very useful and there is no reason to believe the media will be hostile (is there?) so a good strike rate is possible.

Where, then, do you start? Press releases (that is notices you send out) can be in the form of routine mentions or more particular stories, but remember that much of the impact of both sorts of material is cumulative. Customers will sometimes comment that 'We seem to see mentions of you pretty regularly', but have difficulty remembering the exact context of what was said or, more likely, written. To achieve this cumulative impact, you need to be constantly on the lookout for opportunities of gaining a mention.

Even routine matters, perhaps the appointment of a new member of staff or a move of offices, may be written up. All that is necessary is, first, to remember to make these announcements and, second, to take a disproportionate amount of care and attention as to how they are made. For instance, the announcement of a staff appointment is much more likely to be printed if there is a photograph with it. This takes a little more organizing, but is well worth the trouble.

Beyond the routine announcement, matters can get a little more complicated. News means exactly that! While it may be of interest to you that the firm has 25 staff, inhabits an 18th century mansion or is reorganizing, a journalist will tend to find it difficult to imagine readers starry-eyed with excitement as they read it in their newspaper or journal. You will have to find something with more of an element of news in it; it may be genuinely different, it may be a first comment on something, but it must have something of real interest about it.

If you become known as a source of good comment, stories and articles, then your press contacts will start to come to you and the whole process may gain continuity and momentum. There is, after all, a world of journalists, editors and others with deadlines to meet, space to fill – and they are often worried about how to do it week after week, or month after month. They will certainly respond to some of the ideas that come to them.

Press releases demand that certain conventions are complied with; at least editors will pay more attention to them if they do. This is spelt out below, together with an example of a press release. You should not follow this slavishly: remember that an element of creativity is always necessary.

Composing a press release

There are two, perhaps conflicting aspects of putting together a press release that will stand a good chance of publication. The first is to comply with the 'form' demanded by the newspapers, magazines and journals to whom you send your release; the second is to stand out as being of genuine interest from the very large number of releases received. We'll take the 'form' first:

- It should carry the words 'Press (or News) Release' at the top, together with the date, preferably at the top left-hand side of the first page.
- If an embargo is necessary (ie a request not to publish before a certain date, to ensure news appears as near as possible simult- aneously – as once an item has been in print others will consider it of less interest), it should be clearly stated 'EMBARGO: not to be published before (time) on (date)'. Put this in bold type or use capitals for emphasis.
- Also at the top you need a heading, not too long but long enough to indicate clearly the contents of the release or to generate interest in it.
- Space it out well with wide margins, reasonable gaps between paragraphs and so on. This allows sub-editors to make notes on it.
- If it runs to more than one page make sure it says 'continued' or similar at the foot of the page, even breaking a sentence at the end of the page will make it more likely people will turn over. Similarly, to make it absolutely clear that there is no more, many put 'end' at the foot of the last page.
- Use newspaper style. Short paragraphs. Short sentences. Two short words rather than one long one.
- Keep it brief, long enough to put over the message and on to a second page if necessary, but no more.
- The first sentences are crucial and need to summarize as far as possible the total message.
- Avoid overt 'plugging' (although that may well be what you are doing). Do not mention names, etc right at the beginning, for example.
- Try to stick to facts rather than opinions: an accountant saying 'this event is being arranged for all those who are interested in

minimizing their tax liability', for example, is better than 'this event will be of great interest to all those wanting to minimize their tax liability'.

■ Opinions can be given, in quotes and ascribed to an individual. This works well and can be linked to the attachment of a photograph (which should usually be a black and white print and clearly labelled in case it gets separated from the release).

■ Do not overdo the use of adjectives, which can jeopardize credibility.

■ Avoid underlining things in the text (this is used as an instruction in printing to put words underlined in italics).

■ Separate notes to the publication from the text of the release. You can present them as footnotes, for example, 'photographers will be welcome'. If you don't separate them, they could get printed as part of the story.

■ Never omit from a release, at the end, a clear indication of who can be contacted for further information and their telephone number (even if this is on the heading of the first page).

■ Finally, make sure that it is neat, well typed and presentable and that it lists enclosures. It may be obvious perhaps, but it is important.

So, how do you make your press release stand out? There are fewer rules here, but two points are certainly worth bearing in mind:

■ Don't 'cry wolf'. Save releases for when you really have a story. If you send a series of contrived releases there is a danger that a good one among them will be ignored.

■ Make sure the story sounds interesting and, without overdoing things, be enthusiastic about it. If you are not, why would they be? Perhaps the only good thing in the world that is contagious is enthusiasm.

Public relations is an area that can produce not just awareness of your operation, but also paint a particular picture of it. It can create not only understanding, but a positive interest in your firm that whets the appetite for more information, prompts enquiries, re-establishes dormant contacts and reinforces your image with existing customers. An example of a press release is shown in Figure 2.1.

Not only is public relations activity a powerful weapon in your promotional armoury, it is also free. Well, it seems free when

Creativity & Commitment

Sandra Hewett
Media Relations
104–110 Goswell Road
London EC1V 7DH

Tel: 020 7689 3116
Fax: 020 7689 3188
e-mail: info@shmr.co.uk

13 May 1999

NEVILLE JOHNSON OFFICES
IN MANAGEMENT BUYOUT

The management team of Neville Johnson Offices (NJO), led by Managing Director Tony Barry, has today (13 May) agreed the terms of a management buyout (MBO) of the company they have run for ten years. NJO is the UK market leader in the manufacture and installation of home office furniture. The deal is worth £8 million and was led by venture capital company 3i, providing £3.6 million together with funds under management. Subject to shareholder approval, completion will take place on 28 May.

The buyout was from parent company Calderburn, a small cap listed plc which bought the company in 1994.

The company grew from sales of £3 million, when Tony and Sales Director Nigel Pailing joined, to nearly £10 million currently. They will take the majority share of the management equity while three other members of the team, Finance Director Stephen Proctor, Production Director Keith Holland and UK Sales Manager Jim Gettings, will hold minority stakes.

NJO was the first to identify the home office market and was ideally positioned to exploit the 1990s trend of homeworking, as self-employment and flexible working grew. It has the majority of the

More/...

NJO completes MBO 2/...

home office furniture market which saw around 84% real growth between 1993 and 1998.[1]

Its customer is the discerning individual at the top end of the market, who appreciates its reputation for quality and customer care. The company has also successfully transferred this reputation to commercial offices, with a range designed by one of the most highly respected names in the industry.

The company's market position has been gained by extensive advertising in the Sunday supplements. Tony Barry says that future growth will come from both new media and new market exploitation. They now have their sights set on the European market.

Grant Thornton and Berwin Leighton advised the management team of NJO. Osborne Clarke provided legal advice to 3i.

Ends

For more information, please contact:

Tony Barry, Managing Director, Neville Johnson Office 0161 848 1207
Sandra Hewett, Sandra Hewett Media Relations 020 7721 7692

Note for editors:
Neville Johnson Offices is the country's market leader in home office furniture. It was founded in 1988 and is now owned by its management team, led by Tony Barry and Nigel Pailing.

---

[1] Source: Mintel
Note: Thanks to Sandra Hewett for permission to reproduce this example.

Figure 2.1 An example of a press release

compared with advertising, which is communication in bought space, but there is a catch. It takes time! And in any small business time is certainly money. In too many organizations public relations is neglected because staff are busy, even over-stretched, and opportunities are missed. Yet if the power of public relations is consistently ignored then not only are opportunities missed, but the image that is created by default may actually damage business prospects.

In many ways, therefore, time spent on public relations is time well spent, and often more in terms of relationships than resources. It is an area in which you should leave no stone unturned, since many things can have a PR effect and some of the more personal ones give rise to sales opportunities. Consider whether you can find openings to:

- speak at a conference;
- write an article;
- judge some competition;
- belong to something where you will meet the right people (a trade or professional body, maybe);
- sponsor something/someone;
- sit on or chair a committee.

Don't reject such things out of hand. There are many small companies using such methods and gaining advantage from them. All it takes is time, effort (and confidence) to set them up. You will not succeed with everything like this you try, indeed you will not succeed first time with many of your efforts, but some will work. The first step is to be observant and spot opportunities: public relations (like most promotion) is in part a state of mind.

While you cannot rely on public relations for the total promotional job that is necessary, it can and should provide a sound foundation for promotion. It is specifically suitable when budgets are low and can work effectively in tandem with advertising and other techniques to create the right overall impact. Advertising, which we turn to next, cannot by definition be a prime promotional tactic if budgets are limited, but if well conceived and used selectively it can play a crucial role in the total mix.

ADVERTISING

First, here is a definition. Advertising is 'any paid form of non-personal communication directed at target audiences through various media in order to present and promote products, services and ideas'. More simply, it can be called 'salesmanship in print or film'.

The role of advertising, as one of a number of variable elements in the communication mix, is 'to sell or assist the sale of the maximum amount of the product or service, for the minimum cost outlay'.

There is a variety of forms of advertising, depending on the role it is called upon to play among the other marketing techniques employed, in terms of both the type of advertising and the target to which it is directed. These include, by way of example:

- national advertising;
- retail or local advertising;
- direct mail advertising (dealt with in detail in Chapter 3);
- advertising to obtain leads for sales staff;
- trade advertising;
- industrial advertising.

A more specific way of understanding what advertising can do is to summarize some of the major purposes of advertising – that is, the objectives that can be achieved through using advertising in particular ways. Here is a representative list:

- to inform potential customers of a new product/service;
- to increase the frequency of use;
- to increase the use of a product/service;
- to increase the quantity purchased;
- to increase the frequency of replacement;
- to lengthen the buying season;
- to present a promotional programme;
- to bring a family of products together;
- to turn a disadvantage into an advantage;
- to attract a new generation of customers;
- to support or influence a franchise dealer, agent or intermediary;
- to reduce brand substitution by maintaining brand loyalty;
- to make known the organization behind the product/service (corporate image advertising);

- to stimulate enquiries;
- to give reasons why wholesalers and retailers should stock or promote a product;
- to provide technical information about a product/service.

There are clearly many reasons behind the advertising that you see around you. These reasons are not mutually exclusive and many of those listed could apply to your business, though an advertisement that majors on one (or few) objectives is perhaps more likely to be successful than one with widely disparate aims. Whatever specific objectives the use of advertising seeks to achieve, the main purpose is usually to:

- gain the customer's interest;
- attract customer interest;
- create desire for the product or service; and
- prompt the customer to buy.

Advertising is, therefore, primarily concerned with attitudes and attitude change; creating favourable attitudes towards a product or service should be an important part of the advertising effort. Fundamentally, however, advertising also aims to sell, usually with the minimum of delay, although a longer time period may be needed in the case of informative or corporate (image building) advertising.

Any advertisement should relate to the product or service, its market and potential market and, as a communicator, it can perform a variety of tasks:

- *It can provide information.* This information can act as a reminder to current users of the product's existence.
- *It can attempt to persuade.* It can attempt to persuade current users to purchase again, non-users to try the product for the first time and new users to change brands or suppliers.
- *It can create cognitive dissonance.* This means advertising can help to create uncertainty about the ability of current suppliers to best satisfy a need. In this way, advertising can effectively persuade customers to try an alternative product or brand. (Extreme versions of this would appear to come under the heading 'knocking copy' – used sometimes by, among others, car manufacturers.)
- *It can create reinforcement.* Advertising can compete with competitors' advertising, which itself aims to create dissonance,

to reinforce the idea that current purchases best satisfy the customers' needs.

Moreover, advertising may aim to reduce the uncertainty felt by customers immediately following an important and valuable purchase, when they are debating whether or not they have made the correct choice.

Media and methods

There are, of course, many forms of advertising and perhaps the simplest is the entry in *Yellow Pages*. Incidentally, with directories, the rule is to go into anything and everything which offers a free entry (after all, you never know) and think long and hard about *everything* else. Some may, in a particular industry, be vital; others are, let us say, questionable. This kind of advertising often appears as what is usually called a 'tombstone' advertisement:

> J BLOGGS & CO
> **Pet food/products**
> 64 High Street
> Oxbridge

This tells you what they do, just, but no more. Something has to be added if it is to stand out among other, similar ads on the page:

> J BLOGGS & CO
> **Pet food/products**
> 64 High Street
> Oxbridge
> **A free canary with every packet of seed**

Just adding one line makes a difference, but a headline might do more. (See page 97.)

What other media are there? The answer is that they are many and various and each is read or seen by a different mix of people; there are advertisements on books of matches and there has been an advertisement on the space shuttle. The possibility of finding media that correspond with the profile of the customer group you are targeting is high:

- *Daily newspapers.* These often enjoy reader loyalty and hence high credibility. Consequently, they are particularly useful for prestige and reminder advertising. As they are read hurriedly by many people, lengthy copy may be wasted.
- *Sunday newspapers.* These are read at a more leisurely pace and consequently greater detail can be included.
- *Colour supplements.* These are ideal forums for advertising, but appeal to a relatively limited audience.
- *Magazines.* These vary from quarterlies to weeklies and from very general, wide-coverage journals to very specialized interests. Similarly, different magazines of the same type (eg fashion) appeal to different age and social-economic groups. Magazines are normally colourful and are often read on a regular basis.
- *Local newspapers.* These are particularly useful for anything local, but are relatively expensive if used for a national campaign. They are sometimes used for advertising support if you are test marketing in one or two specific areas.
- *Television.* This is regarded as the best overall medium for achieving mass impact and creating an immediate or quick sales response. It is arguable whether or not the audience is captive or receptive, but the fact that television is being used is often sufficient in itself to generate trade support. Television allows the product to be demonstrated and is useful in test marketing new products because of its regional nature. It is very expensive.
- *Outdoor advertising.* This lacks many of the attributes of press and television, but is useful for reminder copy and as a support role in a campaign. Strategically placed posters near busy thoroughfares or at commuter stations can offer very effective long-life support advertising.
- *Exhibitions.* These generate high impact at the time of the exhibition but, except for very specialized ones, their coverage of the potential market is low. They can, however, perform a useful long-term 'prestige' role and prompt specific enquires (see Chapter 5).

- *Cinema.* With its escapist atmosphere, this can have an enormous impact on its audience of predominantly young people; but without repetition (ie people visiting the cinema once every week) it has little lasting effect. It is again useful for backing up press and television, but for certain products only, bearing in mind the audience and the atmosphere.
- *Commercial radio.* Use of this medium offers repetition and has proved an excellent outlet for certain products. It is becoming apparent that the new local radio stations appeal to a wide cross-section of people and thus offer 'support' potential to a whole range of products.
- *Web sites.* These, an aspect of the Internet revolution, are increasingly used, often as a form of advertising, sometimes linked to a facility for customers to order (e-commerce). As a short digression to this chapter, the section below sets out some key principles about the role of Web sites and how to use them.

Web sites

Technology has a way of creeping up on you. One day the Internet is an uncertain prediction, now we are all learning to surf and references to e-commerce are all around. You may have bought this book by contacting a Web site (Kogan Page has one: www.kogan-page.co.uk) and many businesses of all sorts, even small ones, have their own Web site. Indeed, to create something simple is now a classic low cost option.

It is not my purpose here to explain the technology, indeed I am hardly qualified to do so. However, a Web site is no more than a new option in the promotional mix and needs to be considered accordingly. Setting up a Web site can be time-consuming and expensive; so too can maintaining it and keeping it up to date. Some businesses acted very early as technology created this opportunity; some acted solely because it was 'something that had to be done', perhaps to keep up with others, perhaps to pander to the ego of someone involved and enthusiastic. Whatever the reason it was sometimes ill considered and time and money were spent to no good effect. Whatever might be done needs thinking through; the first question is very obvious and straightforward.

What objectives do you have for your Web site?

There may be several, but they should all be specific. It is important to know whether the cost of setting this up is delivering what was intended; important, not least, to how the site is developed. Perhaps the site is in part a source of reference. You want people to consult it to obtain information (and be impressed by it at the same time). This may save time and effort expended in other ways. Perhaps you intend that it plays a more integral part in the selling process, and you want to measure its effectiveness in terms of counting the number of new contacts it produces and, in turn, how many of those are turned into actual revenue-producing customers.

So, if you already have a Web site, check whether you have good feedback on its use and the specific results it brings you (for example, counting new contacts or money coming from new customers). Similarly, if you are in the process of setting up a site, ensure consideration of its effectiveness is an inherent part of the process.

In addition, you may have products you want people to order and pay for through direct contact with the site. A consultant might offer a survey of some sort, primarily to put an example of their expertise and style in the hands of prospective clients (though it might also be a source of revenue). In this case not only must the ordering system work well, and this means it must be quick and easy for whoever is doing the ordering, but the follow-up must be good too. Any initial good impression given will quickly evaporate if whatever is ordered takes forever to arrive or needs several chasers. One hazard to good service is to demand too much information as an order is placed. Of course, this kind of contact represents an opportunity to create a useful database, but turning ordering into the Spanish Inquisition will hardly endear you to people.

Whatever objectives are decided upon, there are three distinct tasks. They are to:

- *attract people to the site.* Just having the site set up does not mean people will log on to it in droves, much less the people you really want to attract. Other aspects of promotion must draw attention to it and this may vary from simply having the Web site address on your letterhead to incorporating mention (and perhaps demonstration) of it into customer events.
- *impress people when they see it.* Both with its content and its presentation. This means keeping a close eye on the customers'

view and the practicalities as it is set up. For example, all sorts of impressive graphics and pictures are possible and can look creative and may well impress. Certainly you will need some. But such devices take a long time to download, and if that is what you are encouraging people to do they may find this tedious, especially if the graphics seem more like window dressing than something that enhances the content in a useful way.

■ _encourage repeat use._ This may or may not be one of the objectives. If it is then efforts have to be made to encourage re-contacting and this too may involve an overlap with other forms of communication.

Beyond this you also need to consider carefully:

■ what the content should be (this is an ongoing job, not a one off);
■ how contacting the Web site can prompt a dialogue;
■ how topical it should be (this affects how regularly it needs revision);
■ its convenience and accessibility (it will need a suitable navigation mechanism);
■ whether it looks consistent (and not as if it has been put together by committee);
■ the protection it needs (is anything confidential, is it vulnerable to hackers, etc?)

Overall, it will need the same planning, co-ordination and careful execution as any other form of marketing communication. In addition, it is likely to necessitate active, ongoing co-operation from numbers of people around the firm who will provide and update information. Given how difficult it can be to get even a small group of people to agree on one page of copy for a new brochure, this may present quite a challenge. Clearly responsibility for the site and what it contains must unequivocally be laid at someone's door, together with the appropriate authority to see it through.

In addition, someone needs to have the necessary technical knowledge. This may be internal or external, but it needs to be linked to an understanding of marketing and/or the ability to accept a clear brief. This is not a case of applying all the available technology, building in every bell and whistle simply because it is possible. Practical solutions are necessary to meet clear objectives.

If a site is to be useful, that is, an effective part of the marketing mix, then sufficient time and effort must be put in to get it right. And the ongoing job of maintaining it must be borne in mind from the beginning.

A link with research

An interesting and practical development is the availability of standard, cost-effective software packages that can work as an integral part of a Web site and monitor how it is used. In fact, there are now such add-ons better described as research tools. One such, *ONQUEST*, not only allows regular research and formal monthly analysis of exactly who is using a Web site, their precise character-istics, and how and why they are in touch with the site, but it also allows the way the system works to be simply tailored to the needs and objectives of an individual firm. The intention is to obtain information that will make the Web site a more accurate and effective marketing tool. (Details of the *ONQUEST* system can be obtained from Strategy, Research & Action Ltd, tel 020 8878 9482. The Managing Director, Robin Birn, the researcher who has initiated this development, is familiar with the special nature of small businesses.)

There is a profusion of other technological possibilities. For example, it is possible for someone logged on to a Web site to trigger a phone call from a supplier. Thus you can arrange to be able to talk to a potential customer as they look at your site or afterwards (they may have only one telephone line).

Media selection

Not all media will be appropriate to the nature of any particular business. Media selection is a complex subject best left to experts if advertising is done on any scale, but there is a mix of factors you can consider:

- *Cost.* The greater the exposure the more it costs, so national daily newspapers and TV are unlikely to rank high on your list. Some good rates are available on local commercial radio, however, and this may be worth investigating.
- *Focus.* This means by whom it will be seen. All reputable media are able to provide detailed information regarding their audience.

Look for something where there is a good fit between the group(s) you want to access and those who see the medium, and bear in mind that you pay for *all* the people it addresses – so beware of those that include a much wider span of audience than you need.

■ *Timing.* This can also be important. Some media appear regularly and your ads can feature pretty much when you want – in a local weekly paper, say – while others are less frequent. If timing is important to you, it's worth matching your needs to the medium's frequency: in other words don't easily be persuaded to advertise in a special supplement or advertising feature if its timing doesn't really suit you.

■ *Production factors.* These matter too. Must your advertisement be in colour or not? Does the medium lend itself to photographs and is this important? Will the medium itself provide assistance with design or copywriting (and is that assistance genuinely useful)?

As with everything else, the key question here is not whether something is readily available or affordable, but whether it will actually meet the objectives set and do the job.

Who to target with your advertising

It is often not enough to advertise to consumers alone, particularly where it is important that distributors are willing to stock and promote a product. Even if the sales force plays a prime role in ensuring that stocking and promotion objectives are achieved, *trade advertising* also has an important role to play in this respect:

■ It can remind distributors about the product between selling calls.
■ It can keep distributors fully informed and up to date on developments and changes of policy.
■ It can alleviate problems associated with 'cold-call' selling.

Trade advertising is usually confined to specialist trade publications and the use of direct mail communications from the company to its distributors.

Most trade advertising occurs prior to major consumer advertising campaigns to help ensure the buying in of stock in anticipation of the demand created by the consumer advertising. Thus, when new products are launched, or special promotions introduced, trade support is often achieved through special offers ('13 for the price of 12') or increased (introductory) discounts, all of which can be highlighted by trade advertising. This type of advertising can also communicate to the trade the advantages of new products, as well as the timing and 'weight' of advertising support that is to come.

Creating the ads

Assuming that the analysis of the market has led to a sensible choice of media and advertising strategies, these have to be communicated to whoever is going to produce the advertisement. At its best, the advertisement strategy statement is brief and economical and does its job in three paragraphs:

1. The basic proposition – the promise to the client, the statement of benefit, to whom.
2. The 'reason why' or support proof justifying the proposition, the main purpose of which is to render the proposition as convincing as possible.
3. The 'tone of voice' in which the message should be delivered – the image to be projected and frequently the picture the customer has of him or herself, which it could be unwise to disturb and wise to capitalize on.

Putting the message together, writing the words (the 'copy'), selecting illustrations and so on may still be a problem. It helps to approach it in the right way. You will find more detail on copywriting in Chapter 3 on direct mail; the principles for advertising and leaflets are similar.

If you subcontract copywriting, be careful. Most executives, when faced with a rough or initial visual and copy layout, have an automatic subjective response: 'I like it/I don't like it.' And while the creator may attempt to explain that the appraiser is not a member of the target audience, it is obviously difficult to be objective. While an attempt at objectivity must be made, there are few experienced advertising or marketing executives who can say that their 'judgement' has never let them down. Advertising remains as much an art as a science. The questions that you must ask are:

- Does the advertisement match the strategy laid down?
- Does the advertisement gain attention and create awareness?
- Is it likely to create interest and understanding of the advantages of a particular product or service?
- Does it create a desire for the benefits and conviction of the need to buy?
- Is it likely to prompt potential clients to action?

In basic terms: does the advertising communicate? Will people notice it, understand it, believe it, remember it and buy it? The intention and thus 'shape' of a typical advertisement can be summarized as AIDA:

Objectives	Methods
Attention	To create initial attention and persuade prospects to look further, you must be in the right media, take an appropriate space and use a headline or picture to provide a strong first impression.
Interest	Interest is created by involving the prospects, telling them why they will benefit/what problems will be solved, presenting facts to build the case and describing quality.
Desire	To prompt desire within the audience, it must continue to focus on them. Spell out the benefits, enthuse, be clear, simple and credible. Then they start to want more.
Action	A summary may link the overall message to the injunction to act. If possible specify the action you want, make it easy (perhaps offer a choice) and stress why such action is good for the prospect (rather than for you). Keep stressing benefits throughout and consider adding some urgency.

Quoting 'good' advertising is like walking through quicksand. In isolation from its objectives and strategy, its intention may be unclear. An advert that wins awards may sell little; a simple, unsophisticated one may achieve wonders. The following is therefore quoted from my book *Everything you Need to Know about Marketing*, which is designed to demystify marketing in a light-hearted way and takes a less than serious approach without picking an individual, real example (which would almost certainly be unrepresentative). It does show something of the many different approaches possible.

Sometimes the product is such that, with no competition and a perfect match with customers' needs, all the advertisement has to do is say what the product will do for them:

New instant petrol – one spoonful of our additive to one gallon of water produces petrol at 1p a gallon.

If your message is like this, no problem. Persuasion is inherent in the message. But few products are like that. More likely any product will have competition – and it will be very like its competitors. Then you have to say more about it. Or start by thinking of everything about it. You may even say everything about it:

SPLODGE *– the big, wholesome, tasty, non-fattening, instant, easily prepared chocolate pudding for the whole family.*

Or you can stress one factor, thus implying that your competitors' products are lacking in this respect:

SPLODGE *– the easily prepared pudding.*

Customers may know all puddings of this sort are easy to prepare, but they are still likely to conclude yours are easiest. The trouble with this approach is that in a crowded market there are probably puddings already being advertised as 'easily prepared'. And big, wholesome and all the rest for that matter. What then? Well, one way out is to pick another factor ignored by your competitors because it is not essential:

SPLODGE *– the pudding in the ring-pull pack.*

It may be a marginal factor but your advertisement now implies it is important and that the competitors' products are lacking. Alternatively you can pick a characteristic of total irrelevance:

SPLODGE *– the pudding that floats in water.*

If the competition has done all of this then you have only one alternative: you must feature in the advertisement something else, nothing to do with the product. This may necessitate giving something away:

> **SPLODGE** – *the only pudding sold with a* **free** *sink plunger.*

Or re-packaging:

> **SPLODGE** – *the only pudding in the* **transparent** *ring-pull pack.*

The possibilities are endless and the ultimate goal is always to make your product appear different and attractive, and desirable because of it.

Advertising has to be made to look attractive. Sometimes this may be achieved through added humour, personalities and whatever, or through lavish production values. Some television commercials cost far more per minute than the programmes they punctuate, and the photographic and editing values of the international advertising of big brands like Coca-Cola are clear to all. A danger here is that the pluses may hide the message; viewers of a poster, say, laugh at its humour but cannot recall what the brand name was on it.

Advertising can be expensive, so we will conclude this chapter with some examples of small-scale advertising that can prove effective, especially on a local basis:

■ *Advertisements,* for example posters in other business premises (a typing service advertised on a university noticeboard, a nearby bookshop advertised in a café, even if you have to provide the noticeboard). Here you may need to return the favour (for example, advertise the café in your bookshop), if this is organized on a swap basis.
■ *Posters,* very few and very local – to help people find you (works well, for example, at a station, bus stop or in a car park).

- *'Ads' with the product*, a bookmark with books or card to request a catalogue, paper and plastic bags.
- *Something that can easily be filed away* (like the cards posted through letterboxes advertising taxis or plumbers).
- *Sponsored litterbins*, around the locality.

Sponsorship can be useful. It is worth thinking about all those organizations in your locality that are related in some way to the nature of your business that might help. These could be charities, associations, non-competitive businesses, even local authorities or official and professional bodies. All can be useful, particularly if their activity overlaps with your own in a clear manner. For example, an accountant might sponsor the mathematics prize at a local school as a way of being visible to parents in the area. Again, the only proviso is that the opportunity should link specifically to the business. It is all too easy to confuse cleverness of ideas with clarity of intention.

For all these and any other advertising opportunities you may think of, the trick is to choose what you do carefully and make sure it works hard. Fewer advertisements, well executed, may be better than more ads that have money – and creativity – spread thinly. However, with a little advertising and certainly with an ongoing public relations activity running, visibility should start to build up and you have the beginnings of the promotional 'best buy' for the smaller company. To this we can add various promotional techniques; these are reviewed in the next two chapters.

3

Promotion by Post

Using direct mail effectively

What is written without effort is in general read without pleasure.
SAMUEL JOHNSON

What form of promotion is lowest cost, smallest scale and ideally suited to low-budget marketing? The answer may well be the subject of this chapter: direct mail. Of course it will, in fact, do many things: prompting business from prospects, maintaining business from existing customers and much in between.

First things first: direct mail is only a particular form of advertising – promotion by post. The term encompasses all the elements of the promotional message delivered in this way: brochures, letters, envelopes and how to orchestrate a persuasive message and create a direct mail 'shot' or entire campaign.

The nature of direct mail is a little different from other forms of promotion and there is one particular aspect that is worth a word or two before we go further: its ability to rouse strong feelings, not all of them complimentary. Everyone appears to know someone who has been mailed about something inappropriate and addressed wrongly as 'Dear Madam' when the recipient is a man, and vice versa. Despite this it is used, and used successfully, by a wide range of companies of all sorts, most of them perfectly respectable. Such companies include charities, accountants and publishers, as well as producers of a wide range of products and services, in organizations large and small.

Used effectively, it can produce good results. Further, direct mail – which can be any number of 'shots': 40, 400, 4,000 or 40,000 – has a flexibility that's ideal for the smaller business. Carried out selectively and progressively, it can certainly be cost-effective.

Some very simple, low cost approaches are possible. For example, as I was thinking about this chapter the postcard shown in Figure 3.1 arrived. This is a good 'reminder' promotion, addressed to people known to and knowing the product. In this case it keeps a particular (and quite excellent) management conference centre in the mind of the recipient. (This card has pictures linked to Christmas events, others have used dramatic pictures such as a striking close-up of a rare breed of pig raised in the grounds.) Another recent promotional postcard consisted solely of an invitation to visit a Web site (and made it sound a useful thing to do).

To increase the distinctive nature of what is sent out, Highgate House has used another idea – it prints everything in smart, dark brown ink which, matched to its letterheads and other material, produces a different, yet professional, look. This is a nice touch, which costs very little. In seeking permission to reproduce the card here, I discovered it pulls a good response and helps build the business for all three venues in the Sundial Group.

WHAT MAKES DIRECT MAIL SUCCESSFUL?

Direct mail, whether simple or more complex, has to be approached in the right way. What makes it successful? The answer, in a few words, is attention to detail. As Samuel Johnson, quoted at the start of this chapter, said, 'What is written without effort is generally read without pleasure' – and it's not just words, everything matters: whom you mail, what you send, how the message is put over and the way in which customers are asked to respond. We will review these matters in turn, then look at some examples.

Private Meetings and Private Dining with **Sundial**

 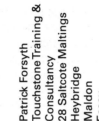

Barnett Hill, Guildford   Woodside, Kenilworth   Highgate House, Northampton

The Sundial Group has an established reputation that extends beyond conference facilities and accommodation to incorporate distinctive hospitality.

The three Sundial venues, Highgate House in Northamptonshire, Barnett Hill in Surrey and Woodside in Warwickshire, are offering customers the opportunity to sample this outstanding hospitality on a non-residential basis. Meeting space and exclusive use of our private dining rooms are now available for business lunches, dinners, board meetings and presentations.

Whether you require the grand setting of Highgate House's magnificent Baronial Hall, the cosy atmosphere of Barnett Hill's Library or the bright versatility of Woodside's Conservatory, the professionalism and dedication of our staff will ensure that you enjoy a truly memorable occasion.

**Call now for Christmas availability
01604 731731**

Patrick Forsyth
Touchstone Training &
Consultancy
28 Saltcote Maltings
Heybridge
Maldon
Essex
CM9 4QP

SUNDIAL
Conference and
training group

Sundial Conference and Training Group
Highgate House
Creaton
Northamptonshire
NN6 8NN

T 01604 731731
F 01604 731777
E info@sundialgroup.com
www.sundialgroup.com

Should you wish your name to be deleted from our database, please write to us at Sundial Conference
and Training Group, Freepost NH4268, Creaton, Northampton NN6 8BR, including this card. Thank you.

CM/1099

Figure 3.1 An example of a personalized 'reminder' promotion

Prospects – selecting respondents

You will always get better results if your mail shots are addressed to individual prospects and that means by name, not along the lines of 'The Managing Director, ABC Co. Ltd'.

The effectiveness of any mailing is clearly dependent on mailing the right people, ie on the quality of the mailing list. There are two separate approaches to the question of lists: either build your own or use other people's (or a combination of both, as they are not mutually exclusive).

Outside sources of lists abound, available most often for rent, sometimes for outright purchase. Rented lists are well guarded and will always include what are called 'seeded names', that is names placed in the list to allow the owner to monitor how it is used. These might include the home addresses of certain members of the renter's staff. This prevents lists hired for one-time use being copied and used again. Using outside lists can be very useful, not least because it avoids the problem of holding them, printing off labels and much of the administrative detail involved. Sources of lists are well documented (the *Direct Mail Databook* is a good reference, for example).

At the same time informal sources, ranging from companies you know to Chambers of Commerce, may also be useful. In addition, you can cull names from a wealth of directories (those that do not make their entries available in list form), not simply to mail once, but to record and use again. For many the most valuable sector of their list is not prospects but actual customers.

Holding and maintaining lists

Mailing lists are a perishable commodity. They have to be maintained and updated. People move jobs, position and location and like to be addressed correctly.

The simplest form of list maintenance is a card index and for some small lists this may be quite adequate. Beyond this some settle for lists on A4 sheets that can be photocopied direct on to sheets of labels, though computers have made many a labelling system obsolete. For all practical purposes – and for any real quantity – list holding now necessitates a computer. As a result most, even quite small, systems are able to hold lists and can be programmed with additional facilities (for instance, mail-merging systems which allow letters to be produced with the name on the label used in the letter).

Computer and software companies and their distributors will be only too willing to offer help and advice. If you have an existing system, the new element must be compatible with it and, while there is a profusion of good standard software available, it is important that this will give you the exact operation you want. For example, you may want to:

- print out by company/organization as well as individual names;
- rebate-sort, ie to deliver post to the Post Office pre-sorted in a way that qualifies for lower rates (though note that it also takes longer to deliver);
- link into other record systems, clients, debtors, etc;
- print quietly or at a certain speed; or
- simply avoid your labels looking as if they have come off a computer system.

All the caveats of purchasing this sort of equipment apply. Like all such systems, exactly what will suit you needs some investigation if you are to end up with something truly suitable. Even when you do, then as the saying has it, 'When your system works well, it's obsolete'. I make no attempt here to itemize specific equipment or software, as what is available changes while you watch. But this is no excuse not to make a decision to buy. However long you wait, there will always be a better system available tomorrow.

A clear intention

The first step, before any mail shot or campaign can be put together, is for you to decide the objectives. What are you looking to prompt? You may say that the answer to this is obvious: you want to sell the firm and its product/services and you want people to buy them. However, this may prove too simplistic a view to enable the construction of an effective mail shot. Promotion may be designed to sell the product, but it is just as likely to be designed to produce:

- enquiries;
- requests for information;
- something that will receive a personal sales follow-up.

To prompt specific action you must be clear exactly what the product/ service is. It is difficult to move from a general description such as 'We provide market research services' to truly descriptive copy, much less persuasive copy. You must be able to see your company from the customers' point of view.

Knowing how and why customers view you as they do is a prerequisite to putting any promotional material together, especially material for direct mail, which may be distributed widely and contain elements that are retained by recipients or used regularly for some time.

A specific response

Having clear objectives for promotion includes having a clear idea what response is looked for from those receiving the mailing. Put simply, what do you want recipients to do if they are interested?

One action (of yours) should be mentioned first. That action is telephone follow-up. It is often very effective to say in your letter, 'I will telephone you in a few days' and then take the initiative (especially when a meeting is the next stage). Otherwise, the need is to offer other options of response which will appeal and appeal sufficiently to prompt the recipient to take the initiative.

The temptation is perhaps to go for simplicity – you ring us; or for what you want most – come and see us for a discussion. The more persuasive you feel your message is, the stronger this temptation may be. Yet the same principle of empathy must be applied. The response (or responses – many direct mail shots provide a choice) must be made attractive in the customers' terms. Will they want to send for more information? If so, how much information should we give them now (without solving the problem) and in what form? Will they want to meet us? If so, whom? Where – our offices, theirs, or a neutral venue? Alone, with others – their colleagues, others with similar interests, ie would they expect or like to attend an event? Even minor details are important. For example, they may be more likely to phone you if you pay for the call or have a freephone number, or to return a card if the postage is pre-paid.

Even if you plan only small-scale direct mail (and this may be worth targeting: 'I will send 10 letters every week', day or month), you must consider all the elements of the direct mail campaign.

THE ELEMENTS OF THE MAIL SHOT

There are four elements to what is sent out:

1. brochures or leaflets;
2. a covering letter;
3. a reply facility; and
4. an envelope.

While the envelope is always necessary (unless you use postcards), the other components can be varied. A 'shot' might consist only of a letter, or only of a brochure, or of a brochure that incorporates a reply coupon; or it might be more elaborate: a letter plus two or three brochures and a reply form and a return envelope. Clearly, many permutations are possible. Together the package must carry the total message and that message must be sufficiently persuasive to prompt action from a number of recipients, which will make the whole exercise cost-effective.

The word 'mail shot' implies one such mailing, while a 'campaign' implies a number of shots over time, which may be about different elements of the range, separate except that they are clearly from the same source. Alternatively, shots may be closer and linked, meaning virtually one message stretched across, say, two separate entities, so that repetition reinforces its impact.

As the way things are done generally relates to more than one element or indeed to the package as a whole, in this section we look at the basic considerations regarding each element: the envelope, brochures and leaflets, the covering letter, and the reply device. The process of putting the promotion together creatively is examined separately later, revisiting some of the elements.

In every case a range of possible approaches, styles and details are identified. Any mail shot using them all would simply submerge under its own gimmicks and become self-defeating. Each does have its place, however and, carefully orchestrated, various combinations can be very effective. It is perhaps important not to take a censorious line in considering them. Of course, there are dangers of inappropriate approaches, but bear the customer in mind and remember that what one person finds pushy another finds persuasive. What matters ultimately is what causes a satisfactory response and nothing that does so in a way customers find acceptable should be over-looked. Remember, also, that the many detailed factors involved in the package build up a number of points, which individually seem of little significance but may together increase the response rate noticeably. That said, let's start by taking a look at what the recipient sees first.

The envelope

This must be serviceable. This sounds obvious, but if there are a number of enclosures the envelope must get them to their destination unscathed. Some feel quality directly affects response rates, believing that a white envelope is better than a manila one. Like many of the possible permutations that are being reviewed this can be tested (see 'Measuring results' later in this chapter).

An 'If undelivered return to (address)' message can be included. This may help to avoid waste and prompt updates to the list by identifying when things are wrongly addressed.

Of course, some business recipients will not see the envelopes, as their secretaries will open the mail. But some will and some secretaries will clip an informative envelope to the contents before passing it on. So you may consider having the first part of the message printed on the envelope. The purpose of the envelope carrying such a message is not so much to help ensure they are opened (research shows that most are), it is more to influence the frame of mind in which they are opened, aiming to generate some, albeit small, interest even at this early stage. If such a message is appropriate it may be complete in itself: 'Details enclosed of how to reduce your tax bill'; questioning: 'Do you want to pay less tax?'; or leave more to be explained by the contents: 'A way to save money... details inside'.

Other devices are possible. For example, a window envelope may show a glimpse of the contents, colour may add to the effect and reflect a corporate colour used inside. Post Office regulations specify how much and what form of printing is allowed on the envelope. In the UK, the Post Office guide, *Go Direct*, is the best reference to these issues and regulations.

Brochures and leaflets

These may be items used elsewhere: brochures sales people distribute or leaflets you display in reception. However, such material may be unsuitable for a mail shot and you may need to produce new material, tailored specifically to the job in hand.

In either case, the brochure is unlikely always to set out to tell people 'everything there is to know about the firm'; rather, it may prompt a desire for discussion. Too much information can even have the reverse effect. One hotel, sending direct mail to prompt conference business, found that the numbers of potential clients coming to inspect the hotel doubled when they replaced a short letter and glossy comprehensive brochure with a longer letter, no brochure and an invitation.

The production of brochures generally is an area of increasing professionalism and great care is needed in defining the objective, creating the right message and making sure the brochure looks good and reflects the image the firm intends to project. The days of the bland, general brochure, very similar to those of other firms, describing the chronological history of the firm and everything it does, and intended to be used for everything, are rapidly passing. What is needed now is the ability to match each objective in each particular area with something specifically designed for the job. This may mean producing separate brochures for each product. It may mean that any 'corporate' brochure is a folder with separate inserts aimed at different target groups or different types of customer. It may mean a revised brochure every year. It may even mean a difference between the sort of brochure that is right to give a prospective customer after a preliminary meeting and the sort that is suitable to present to an intermediary who may have a role in, say, recommending you to others. It's 'horses for courses'.

For direct mail purposes the brochure or leaflet concerned must be specific to the objective set for the particular promotion. Brochures may need to be reasonably self-standing: after all, they may get separated from the covering letter, but the total content – letter plus brochure – needs to hang together, to produce a complete and integrated message.

What must be created is something that is accurately directed at a specific group, with a clear objective in mind and – above all – that is persuasive. This may seem obvious: of course promotional material is there to inform, but it must do so persuasively. That is the prime purpose. But this does not mean moving to something that is inappropriately strident (which might in any case be self-defeating); it *does* mean putting a clear emphasis on customer need and benefits (what things do for people, rather than what they are). Essentially, a less introspective approach, better designed to its purpose, is the rule. What does this mean?

There are a few rules to be observed about brochures and they are designed to be broken. This is because brochures must be *creatively* constructed to reflect the image of the firm graphically, differentiate it from its competitors and aim their chosen message directly at the target group addressed.

The covering letter

This is a crucial element to get right and there are several factors to consider.

The right appearance

Basics first. It must look right. It must be attractively laid out, grammatically correct and well presented (even the choice of paper quality can be significant). In selling a service this is especially important since it gives the impression that it has originated in an efficient and reputable firm.

The letterhead itself is important to the image: up to date yet not 'over the top' is what should be aimed at, but this is not easy. Subjective judgements are involved. Ultimately, it is a matter of opinion and in smaller firms this can sometimes mean a safe compromise which may dilute impact. Consider, too, whether your standard letterhead is right for direct mail.

An appropriate salutation

The salutation is the next important item to consider. Numbers may preclude individual salutations. If you are not saying 'Dear Mr Smith', or 'Dear John', what do you say? One answer is nothing. Simply start with a heading. Doing so does not preclude you finishing with your name, though in this case you should omit 'Yours sincerely' and set the name close enough to the text, so that it does not look as if the signature was forgotten, or including the signature (or signatures) in order to give a personal touch. If you are only mailing small quantities you can actually sign each letter. On other occasions a standardized opening may be necessary, for example:

Dear Client or Customer (that at least is clear)
Dear Sir
Dear Reader
Dear Colleague
Dear Finance Director (or other appropriate title).

In many ways none of these is taken to be more than a token greeting and, unless it is something really novel, will have comparatively little impact. If you can find a form of appropriate words, use them; almost anything is better than 'Dear Sir/Madam'!

The need for a structure

In selling face-to-face, you can adapt your approach to the individual you are with as the conversation proceeds. In a letter this is not possible and a formula to structure the approach is useful. The classic sales acronym, AIDA (Attention, Interest, Desire, Action), set out in Chapter 2, works well in providing a structure for letters and represents accurately the job to be done in prompting a response.

How letters are read

Before looking at how such a structure helps the composition of the letter, consider for a moment what happens when it is received. People seldom read a letter immediately in the same sequence in which it was written. Their eyes flick from the sender's address to the ending, then to the greeting and the first sentence, skim to the last – and then, if the sender is lucky, back to the first sentence for a more careful reading of the whole letter. Research has shown a clear sequence (see Figure 3.2) so the first sentence is an important element in 'holding' the reader and it should arouse immediate interest.

With that in mind consider the sequence of the letter, looking at it first as a whole. It will, I hope, be clear by now that the copy for the letter, as for the brochure(s) in fact, is crucial. You are unlikely to be able to dictate it straightaway, certainly not to begin with.

A letter will need thinking about and planning and it will probably go through a number of drafts. Write down the key points, headings, identify the main benefits – create a skeleton. Then, with some guidelines in mind, you can look at how it all goes together.

①②③ – information, taken in very fast. Who is it from?
④ – if there is one, the PS is the 'most read part of any letter'.
⑤ – an overall scan. Do I have to read it all? Use of headings will affect this view.
⑥ – from beginning on (provided the opening is effective).

Figure 3.2 Letters: reading sequence

Attention – the opening

The most important part of the letter is the start. It may well determine whether the rest of the letter is read. The opening may be quite short, a heading perhaps, a couple of sentences, two paragraphs, but it is disproportionately important. A good start will help as you write the letter, as well as ensuring the recipient reads it. Omit or keep references short and make subject headings to the point – the reader's point. Do not use 'Re:'. Make sure the start of the letter will command attention, gain interest and lead easily into the main text. For example:

- ask a 'Yes' question;
- explain why you are writing to that reader particularly;
- explain why the reader should read the letter;
- flatter the reader (carefully);
- explain what might be lost if the reader ignores the message;
- give the reader some 'mind-bending' news (if you have any).

Interest/desire – the body of the letter

The body of the letter runs straight on from the opening. It must consider the readers' needs or problems from their point of view. It must interest them. It must get them nodding in agreement: 'Yes, I wish you could help me on that.' Of course (you say) you are able to help them. In drafting you must write what you intend for the readers and list the benefits you can offer, not features, and in particular the benefits that will help them solve their problems and satisfy their needs.

You have to anticipate the reader's possible objections to your proposition in order to select your strongest benefits and most convincing answers. If there is a need to counter objections, then you may need to make your letter longer and give proof, for example a quote from a third party that says the benefits are genuine. However, remember to keep the letter as short as possible, but still as long as necessary to complete the case. If that is two, three or more pages, so be it.

It's easy to find yourself quoting the literature that will accompany the letter to the reader. If you were writing a lecture on the subject, you would probably need all that information. When writing to a prospective customer you have to select just the key benefits that will be of particular value to the reader and that support the literature.

The body copy must:

■ keep the reader's immediate interest;
■ develop that interest with the best benefit;
■ win the reader over with a second benefit and then further benefits.

The next job is to ensure action from the reader by a firm close.

Action – the letter ending

In closing you can make a (short) summary of the benefits of the proposition. Having decided on the action you want the reader to take, you must be positive about getting it.

It's necessary to nudge the reader into action with a decisive close. Don't use phrases like these:

'We look forward to hearing...'
'I trust you have given...'
'...favour of your instructions.'
'...doing business with you.'
'I hope I can be of further assistance.'

These are really phrases added as padding between the last point and 'Yours sincerely'. Instead, use real closing phrases. Here are some examples:

The alternative close:

■ ask the reader to telephone or write, using the reply-paid envelope;
■ ask for a meeting or send for more information.

Immediate gain:

■ 'Return the card today and your profitability could be improved.'

'Best' solution:

■ 'You want a system that can cope with occasional off-peak demands, that is easy to operate by semi-skilled staff and is presented in a form that will encourage line managers to use it. The best fit with all these requirements is our system "X". Return the card indicating the best time to install it.'

Direct request:

- ▓ 'post the card today';
- ▓ 'telephone us without delay'.

Consider, too, whose name should appear at the bottom of the letter. Replies will tend to come back to that person – so will queries. So should it be the sales office, one director or another and how well are they able to cope with any response? Make sure the name is typed below the signature, as signatures tend to be awkward to read, and that the job title or name of the department is included. People like to know who they're dealing with.

PS: Remember the power of the postscript. Secretaries will tell you they are for things inadvertently left out, while direct mailers will tell you they get read. Use them for repetition or to add a final benefit – it can add strength to the message.

PPS: Some people even use two!

An appropriate tone

We should also consider the language used in such letters. Many people have acquired a habit of artificiality in writing, approaching it quite differently from their way of talking to a customer. This over-formality can reduce their chances of making a sale.

The language you use is clearly important. It must be clear, appropriate and have sufficient impact to persuade. The checklist below sets out some basic rules for persuasive copy:

Be clear	Make sure that the message is straightforward and uncluttered by 'padding'. Use short words and phrases. Avoid jargon.
Be natural	Don't project yourself differently just because it's in writing.
Be positive	In tone and emphasis (be helpful).
Be courteous	Always.
Be efficient	Project the right image.
Be personal	Use 'I' – say what *you* will do.
Be appreciative	'Thank you' is a good phrase.

The next checklist examines specific aspects of the language used in letters. I hope this is not labouring the point, but some people in smaller businesses who have no training in marketing and with a strong background in, say, the technicalities of what they do, can have a tendency towards gobbledegook. I recently saw a note tabled at a board meeting on recommendations proposed by a broker about pension schemes. After a long silence someone said, 'I don't understand it', immediately joined by a chorus of 'Neither do I.' This must not be the general reaction to the material contained in your direct mail. You should:

- *Avoid trite openings:*
  We respectfully suggest...
  We have pleasure in attaching...
  Referring to the attached...
  This letter is for the purposes of requesting....
- *Avoid pomposity:*
  We beg to advise...
  The position with regard to...
  It will be appreciated that...
  It is suggested that the reasons...
  The undersigned/writer...
  May we take this opportunity to...
  Allow me to say in this instance...
  Having regard to the fact that...
  We should point out that...
  Answering in the affirmative/negative...
  We are not in a position to...
  The opportunity is taken to mention...
  Dispatched under separate cover....
- *Avoid coldness and bad psychology:*
  Advise/inform
  Desire
  Learn/note
  Obtain
  Regret
  Trust.
- *Avoid clichéd endings:*
  Thanking you in advance...
  Assuring you of our best attention at all times, we remain...
  Trusting we may be favoured with...

Awaiting a favourable reply...
Please do not hesitate to....
■ *Keep it simple – prefer short words to long:*
Approximately becomes *about*.
Commencement becomes *start*.
Elucidate becomes *explain*.
Considerable becomes *great*.
■ *Prefer one or two words to several:*
At this moment in time becomes *now*.
Due to the fact that becomes *because*.
In the not too distant future becomes *soon*.
There can be no doubt about becomes *it is certain*.
Should the situation arise becomes *if*.

Overall, aim for short sentences, although I'm not suggesting that every sentence should be only four words long. In fact, a mix of longer and shorter sentences works well. This paragraph illustrates this.

Ditto short paragraphs.

Aim for an overall effect that sounds right read out loud. Try it. Get a colleague to read your draft to you. Amend it. Sleep on it. Get it read again. There is no shame in taking a few moments to get such an important piece of writing right. For more about techniques that help actually get words down on paper you could try my book, *How to Be Better at Writing Reports and Proposals*.

Presentation

Finally, remember that the end product should be neatly presented, in a way that the reader finds convenient. So, to make the finishing touches and add impact you should think about the following:

■ Position the letter on the page according to the amount of the text. It is unattractive if there is a huge expanse of white below a very short letter. Position it lower down, in that case, or consider having two sizes of letterhead paper printed and put short letters on the smaller sheets.
■ 'Block' paragraphs, with double spacing between each paragraph for greater clarity and smartness.
■ Leave at least 4 cm at the foot of the page before going on to the second page. Leave a bigger space to avoid having only one or two lines (plus farewells) on the second page.

- Allow enough space for the signature, name and job title. It is better to carry the letter over on to another page than cram it in at the bottom.
- Note, at the foot of the last page, the enclosures mentioned in the text and sent with the letter.
- Staple the pages together to avoid losses, or print letters on A3 paper, folded, to accommodate further pages and produce a quality look.
- Number the pages.
- Number the paragraphs when a lot of points have to be covered.
- Underline all headings or make them **bold**.

Remember, layout of this sort of material cannot be simply left to the secretary or typist. The way a letter is to be presented must be specified by the writer to prevent retyping.

Graphic emphasis can be made with the help of a the word-processor in a number of ways, with:

CAPITALS;
<u>underlining</u>;
   indenting;
bold type;
COLOUR;
italics; and
bold italics.

While these features should not be overdone, they can be useful and, in whatever form and combination you select, need specifying to the typist/typesetter.

Make it easy to reply

Most mailings need some reply device. This may be a coupon, a form to be completed or a self-contained, reply-paid card. Whatever format you select, how it is to be used should be 100 per cent clear. It is fatal to have someone who is interested to the point of taking action being put off because they can't see how to respond.

So, make it clear. Decide what information you want. If you ask for a name and address, adding a request for their job title may make the follow-up just that little bit easier. Let them tick boxes rather than write essays. Let them send their business card rather than filling in anything.

Don't forget to include your telephone number, print it clearly and consider the freephone options. It is certainly a courtesy to use reply-paid letters or cards (or freepost). If you opt for reply-paid, do make it first class, since there is something incongruous about asking for an urgent response and then offering a second-class envelope in which to send it back.

Allow enough time, since there are arrangements to be made and you will need to liaise with the Post Office. The standard reply-paid format seems straightforward, but requires a licence (thereafter you only pay for those that come back) and must conform to the prescribed format in terms of both size and style of printing.

Think carefully before you omit this element of the total package – an easy means of response can make all the difference to your results. And do not treat it as a simple extra – check it carefully and ask someone else if the description of *exactly* what you want done is clear and the method of returning it simple and appropriate.

Here is a final thought, at least for small, specialist mail shots. Actually putting a postage stamp on the reply envelope, rather than using a printed reply-paid format, can *double* your responses. Clearly it costs more, as you pay for all the reply envelopes you send out rather than only those that come back, but the resulting responses may be worth more in the long run.

MEASURING RESULTS

Having touched on the reply vehicle, as this is primarily what provides feedback, it now seems appropriate to pause and consider the monitoring of direct mail activity. One of the advantages of direct mail is its ability to be tested and fine-tuned as a result, easily and at low cost.

The reply card can be coded to the list used, or the mailing material, or both. In other words, different versions of the mailing can be used and a check kept on how responses vary. If different batches of reply cards are produced with variations they can be sorted and checked on receipt. The code may literally be a code, batches A and B (with A or B printed in the corner); or the return address may be varied: Department X or Y and so on. In this way not only can immediate response be measured but, in the longer term, conversion rates can be checked too. It could be that in monitoring two lists one produces twice as many initial responses, but the quality of prospect and conversion rate make it less effective.

In terms of the detail of the mailing, if split runs are used a variety of comparisons may be made. This can be well worth checking and you should never underestimate the difference minor changes – which you may regard as purely cosmetic – can make. For example, you could check factors such as the following, one against the other:

Copy	long *vs* short;
	punchy *vs* conversational.
Colour	one *vs* another;
	black/white *vs* one colour.
Reply vehicle	card *vs* form;
	stamp *vs* reply-paid;
	send business card *vs* fill in form.
Cost	reference to price *vs* not.
Service	specific service *vs* range of services.
Illustrations	include *vs* not;
	photograph *vs* line drawings.
Offering	further information *vs* straight to meeting;
	event as first contact *vs* one-to-one meeting.

In fact, any variable element can be tested in this way, continuously over time. Because this process inevitably makes for complications at origination and production stages, it is often neglected. The possible improvement of results that can be created as this kind of database builds up can, however, make the time and effort involved well worth while.

And what sort of results *can* you expect? Response rates from direct mail vary enormously. In some fields companies make a good living from response rates of less than 1 per cent, while in others up to 50 per cent may be achieved. It is only the relationship between money spent and the revenue generated that ultimately matters and on which success can be judged.

COST AND TIMING

Because there are a variety of elements that make up the total it is essential to work out your costs carefully. Prepare a costing sheet, along the lines of the one shown in Figure 3.3, so that you know in advance what will be involved.

Don't forget the costs incurred after the material has been posted and that prompt, efficient and effective action when a reply is received also costs money.

If you are a first-time direct mail user, talk to the Post Office, which has a number of attractive start-up schemes, including one allowing you to send your first quantity of mail post-free.

As well as keeping a close eye on and a written note of costs, the schedule of timings can also be usefully recorded in calendar style. Copy has to be written, brochures designed and printed, overprinted (rather than plain) envelopes need a longer lead time when ordered and, if you are contracting out the collation, insertion and posting also needs a little time. If you are working back from a planned arrival date – perhaps you want this to be exactly four weeks before a planned event – even the time in the post needs estimating.

Always include yourself on the list, maybe sending one to your own office, one to your home and to the homes of one or two colleagues, so that you can monitor exactly when people receive your promotion. And always circulate material internally well ahead of posting, together with any briefing and a special note to those who will be involved in response action once replies start to arrive. It gives the wrong impression if recipients telephone saying they want more information about something they have seen in a mail shot and the switchboard (or worse still a senior member of staff) can only say, 'What mail shot?' Such 'own goals' must be avoided or the impact is diluted and possible new business may be lost.

A CREATIVE APPROACH

Creativity to order

Creativity is about making things look different. Perhaps in the context of direct mail it is about making things that are essentially

Item	£ Cost overall	£ per 000

Brochure   – copy
            – design
            – printing		

Letter – copy/layout – printing		
Envelopes		
Reply mechanism – design/print		
Reply-paid (estimate)		

Mailing
    – collating
    – stapling
    – folding
    – inserting into envelopes/sealing, etc
    – postage   – first class
                – second class
    – rebate sorting (saving £)		

Split-run, additional cost –
            brochure
            letter
            reply mechanism
            envelopes		

Other enclosures –
              –
              –
Follow-up costs
      – eg brochures
      – publications
Event   – venue
      – catering
      – documentation		

Misc.:		
TOTAL		
Never forget the largest cost may well be your time.		

Figure 3.3 Costing your mailshot

similar appear different. As such there can be no magic formula, either for 'being creative' or, much less, for creating the 'perfect' direct mail promotion. By definition it involves seeking new approaches, rather than slavishly following a format. This section sets out some principles and floats some ideas. But it is essentially concerned with prompting an approach that will focus your thinking in the right way, allow you to devise approaches that will create interest and give you an edge on your competition, rather than 'script' things for you. The ideas are clearly not appropriate for every circumstance and I'm certainly not suggesting that every factor should be built into every promotion. The trick is in finding a fresh approach and a permutation of techniques that will put over your message in a persuasive manner.

Definition of the brief

The overall intention

First make some notes and start by reviewing the whole promotional message rather than one component, like the letter, and get absolutely straight in your mind what the overall message is to be. Ask yourself how what you have to say is new, unique or at least different from the way others may present themselves.

Who exactly is your target audience? And is this a sufficiently discrete group? If you try to appeal to too broad a spectrum of recipients at once you may end up not interesting any of them because your message is not sufficiently specific. Clearly, different approaches, even a different tone, will be necessary for existing customers and ones you are hoping to attract.

You must decide whether you are presenting the organization, a product range, or particular aspects of either, and if it is the latter what aspects you will pick. Is the message of topical relevance? Can you describe it in terms of advantages and benefits? If it includes service, can you describe exactly what this means? What are you going to say about costs? What about value for money? What guarantees, proof and testimonials can you offer? And, bearing in mind that the route to action is also important, how can you make the asked-for action attractive?

Put this down on paper in note form, not aiming for final copy, and try to think objectively about how it will appeal. Does it use the best possible approach? Would it interest *you*? If not, you need to think of additional factors to give it greater strength.

'Hooks'

What are hooks? They are a variety of elements that will generate the interest you want by focusing attention in a particular way. Here are some examples:

Combinations	Featuring two things linked together, eg a budget analysis and action plan (for an accountant) or a computer and printer.
Team response	Something to be responded to by more than one person, eg a meeting designed for the managing director and his finance director to attend together.
Limited offer	Only a limited number can attend/only limited stocks are available.
Status	Offering people the opportunity to be the first with something, such as meeting at a prestige venue, meeting local opinion leaders.
A competition	The prize may be the product, eg something simple like a bottle of Scotch, or more elaborate, like a holiday.
Sponsorship	Linked to an event, perhaps a charitable event, eg, 'Meet us on such and such a date and join us at the local theatre club where we are sponsoring the production of... in the evening.'
Highlight the list source	If you are using someone else's list you can opt to feature the link, eg, 'as a member of...', 'as an investor with...'.
Second chance	Mail people a second time as a 'reminder' or increasing the appeal.

You can also highlight aspects of the overall message. Here are some examples:

Timing	An offer that will give benefit 'before the holidays' or 'by the end of the year'.
Exclusivity	An offer to a select group, eg, 'only for clients', 'only for local business people', 'only for farmers in Sussex'.

Such factors as these are clearly not mutually exclusive. They can be linked, added to and no doubt bettered. No one knows in advance what degree of gimmick will appeal, so be careful, but remember that the recipients will probably take a less censorious view than you of such matters. Some level of experiment may well prove worthwhile, and if you are not prepared to be a pioneer keep a sharp eye on what is done by others.

Finally, keep in mind the things people may obtain from your offering. You need to tell them if they will:

- make more money;
- save money;
- save time, effort or hassle;
- be more secure;
- sort out problems;
- exploit opportunities;
- motivate their staff;
- impress their customers, friends or family;
- persuade others more readily (their bank manager or shareholders).

If they will do it quicker, easier, more cost-effectively or more anything else, say that too. If you believe you provide something of real value, have the courage of your convictions and say so. If reading your promotion does not clearly show the reader you believe in what you have to offer, why should they?

With all this in mind you can begin to get some real copy down on paper. There are two key aspects to this: the words (the tone, language and approach you use) and the structure into which you fit the words to complete the message.

Finding the words

Writing the text

The point about keeping it simple has already been made. It's worth repeating here. So use short words and short sentences.

And short paragraphs.

Don't use too much jargon; at worst this will kill a message stone dead, at best it will dilute the message. But as Bernard Shaw said, 'The only golden rule is that there are no golden rules.' This means do nothing to excess. Sometimes you will need a longer word, a long sentence and some judiciously chosen jargon.

Two other approaches should pervade the text. First, it should be written from the customer's, or potential customer's, point of view. As such, it will say 'you' more then 'I' or 'we' – these are the quickest way to give the text an introspective feel.

Secondly, your text must be positive. It should say 'this is the case', 'this will be what is done' and will rarely say things like 'I think...', 'probably' or 'maybe'.

Experienced direct mailers talk about 'magic' words or at least words that inject a tone that should always be present. Here are some of them:

free	today	timely
guarantee	win	respected
new	easy	special
announcing	save	opportunity
you	at once	low cost
now	unique	fresh

You must not overuse such words or your message will become blatantly over the top, but do not neglect them either. Be careful too not to use words that are so overworked that they have come to mean virtually nothing; for example, now every gadget in the known universe has been described as 'user-friendly', does it have any descriptive power left?

You must keep searching for ways of making your copy perform better. Again, the following guidelines are designed not only to float some examples but also to show the approach you need to cultivate. They are presented in terms of 'dos' and 'don'ts', with no apology for any occasional repetition.

The dos

You should do the following:

■ *Concentrate on facts.* The case you put over must be credible and factual. A clear-cut 'these are all the facts you need to know' approach tends to pay particular dividends in certain businesses, eg professional services.

■ *Use captions.* While pictures, illustrations, photographs and charts can often be regarded as speaking for themselves, they will have more impact if used with a caption. (This can be a good way of achieving acceptable repetition, with a mention in the text and in the caption.)

■ *Use repetition.* Key points can appear more than once, in the leaflet and the letter, even more than once within the letter itself. This applies, of course, especially to benefits repeated for emphasis.

■ *Keep changing the language.* Get yourself a thesaurus. You need to find numbers of ways of saying the same thing in brochures, letters and so on.

■ *Say what is new.* If you have something new, novel – even unique – to say, make sure the reader knows it. Real differentiation can often be lost, so in the quantity of words make sure that the key points still stand out.

■ *Address the recipient.* You must do this accurately and precisely. You must know exactly to whom you are writing, what their needs, likes and dislikes are and be ever conscious of tailoring the message. Going too far towards being all things to all people will dilute the effectiveness for any one recipient.

■ *Keep them reading.* Consider breaking sentences at the end of a page so that readers have to turn over to complete the sentence. (No, it doesn't look quite so nice, but it works.) Always make it clear that other pages follow, putting 'continued...' or similar at the foot of the page.

■ *Link paragraphs.* This is another way to keep them reading. Use 'horse and cart' points to carry the argument along. For instance, one paragraph starts, 'One example of this is...'; the next starts, 'Now let's look at how that works...'

■ *Be descriptive.* Really descriptive. In words, a system may be better described as 'smooth as silk' than 'very straightforward to operate'. Remember, *you* know how good what you are describing is, the readers do not. You need to tell them and you must not assume they will catch your enthusiasm from a brief phrase.

■ *Involve people.* First your own people. Don't say 'The head of our XYZ Division', say, 'John Smith, the head of our XYZ Division.' And other people. Don't say, 'It is a proven service', say, 'More than 300 clients have found it valuable.'

■ *Add credibility.* For example, if you quote users, quote names (with their permission); if you quote figures, quote them specifically and mention people by name. Being specific adds to credibility, so don't say, 'This is described in our booklet on...', rather: 'This is described on page 16 of our booklet on...'

■ *Use repetition.* Key points can appear more than once, in the leaflet and the letter, even more than once within the letter itself. This applies, of course, especially to benefits repeated for emphasis. You will notice this paragraph is repeated, either to show that the technique works or perhaps to demonstrate that half-hearted attempts at humour are not altogether recommended.

The don'ts

You should not:

■ *Be too clever.* It's the argument that should win the reader round, not your flowery phrases, elegant quotations or clever approach.

■ *Be too complicated.* The point about simplicity has been made. It applies equally to the overall argument.

■ *Be pompous.* This means saying too much about you, your organization and your product/services (instead of what it means to the reader). It means writing in a way that is too far removed from the way you would speak. It means following too slavishly the exact grammar at the expense of an easy, flowing style.

■ *Overclaim.* While you should certainly have the courage of your convictions, too many superlatives can become self-defeating. Make one claim that seems doubtful and the whole argument suffers.

■ *Offer opinions.* Or at least not too many compared with the statement of facts, ideally substantiated facts.

■ *Lead into points with negatives.* For example, don't say, 'If this is not the case we will...', rather, 'You will find... or...'

■ *Assume your reader lacks knowledge.* Rather than saying, for example, 'You probably don't know that...', it would be better to say, 'Many people have not yet heard...', or: 'Like others, you probably know...'

■ *Overdo humour.* Never use humour unless you are very sure of it . An inward groan as they read does rather destroy the nodding agreement you are trying to build. A quotation or quip,

particularly if it is relevant, is safer and, even if the humour is not appreciated, the appropriateness may be noted.
- *Use up benefits early.* A direct mail letter must not run out of steam: it must end on a high note and still be talking in terms of benefits even at the end.

Editing

A final comment in this section concerns editing. Edit, edit, edit (more repetition). It is usually easier to start with more copy than you need and edit it back to the correct length, improving it as you go, rather than adding to a short draft. In addition, it may need going over more than once and time spent in 'fine-tuning' is often worth while.

LARGE AND SMALL-SCALE PROMOTIONS – EXAMPLES

To investigate this promotional method further we will consider two examples, both linked to the world of books.

Example 1. One book

Another book I have written for Kogan Page is called *Marketing Professional Services*. This is aimed very specifically at such people as accountants, solicitors, surveyors, architects and stockbrokers – people who, like consultants, sell their expertise. Whatever other publicity went on (and this was organized primarily through the publishers), I wanted to be sure my own clients and contacts in this area knew about the book and, more specifically, that they were prompted to purchase a copy.

The two letters shown in Figure 3.4 were sent from my office together with a small flyer containing an order form. They were mailed three or four weeks apart in the order shown. They worked well. Of those receiving the first letter, 23 per cent ordered. When those remaining who had not ordered were mailed again, 13 per cent ordered. This constitutes about a 33 per cent response from the

28 Saltcote Maltings
Heybridge
Maldon
Essex CM9 4QP

Telephone & Fax: 01621 859300

TRAINING AND CONSULTANCY

A one hundred per cent
biased recommendation

Reflecting the special nature of the professional services sector (it is not at all like selling baked beans or ball bearings), my book '**Marketing Professional Services**' is published this month. <u>It offers practical guidance on how marketing applies to, and can be effectively implemented in, the world of professional services.</u> A review of the original edition described it as:

'**... an informative, accomplished and entertaining guide ... Copious in information, fundamental and practical in advice, this marketing handbook is a convincing and positive guide with a potentially long shelf-life**' (*Practice Marketing* magazine).

The new edition has been sponsored by the Institute of Directors. As an absurdly generous gesture to those in the professions with whom I have had some contact, copies are obtainable from here by return and *post free*.

Details are enclosed. Orders sent here, together with a cheque, will be dealt with on this basis for the next month only.

So, complete and return the form – as they say in all the best promotions – **now**.

Kind regards

PATRICK FORSYTH

June 1999

28 Saltcote Maltings
Heybridge
Maldon
Essex CM9-4QP

Telephone & Fax: 01621 859300

We are making sufficient profit, thank you
– and <u>don't want to make any more.</u>

I am sure you are not, in fact, saying this but you did ignore my last
letter about my book '**Marketing Professional Services**' which was
published last month in a new edition sponsored by the Institute of
Directors. <u>It offers practical guidance on how marketing applies to,</u>
<u>and can be effectively implemented in, the unique world of</u>
<u>professional services.</u> One reviewer of the original edition described
it as:

'… an informative, accomplished and entertaining guide … Copious
in information, fundamental and practical in advice, this marketing
handbook is a convincing and positive guide with a potentially long
shelf-life' (*Practice Marketing* magazine).

You can receive a copy **promptly and post free** – details are again
enclosed. Just return the form with the appropriate remittance and,
who knows, there may well be just a few ideas that can be of help
with your business profitability (if you want).

I hope to hear from you about this and, of course, if I may assist in
any other way do please let me know.

Kind regards

PATRICK FORSYTH

July 1999

Figure 3.4 Two examples of promotional letters

whole list. The numbers were small, but this is very typical of one sort of use of direct mail that is ideal for small businesses. A series of such shots, each focusing on a different product or service, maybe using a series of lists, can be organized progressively throughout the year. In this way the set-up is manageable and a steady flow of orders may result.

Don't be misled by percentages (you never saw a cheque made out with one on!). The numbers that make such promotion viable are not difficult to cost and many people make a good living from responses of only 1 to 2 per cent, or sometimes less. The figures in the case of my letters may not, however, be totally untypical. If you are selling something new, to existing – key – contacts, you would expect a higher response.

The letters themselves make a number of points, which may be of general value:

- They were personalized and addressed to individuals by name.
- They show the use of simple word-processing to achieve graphic emphasis, without overdoing this. A selective use of:
    - headings;
        - indentation;
    - CAPS;
    - <u>underlining</u>;
    - **bold type**;
    - *italics*;
    - quotations, etc,

  will always have greater impact than a solid page of standard text.
- They were designed together to follow one after the other. It is unrealistic to think you will ever obtain 100 per cent response and with many lists (perhaps especially those of known customers) two shots will often be cost-effective – and there are no doubt examples of three, four or more working well.
- A (very) small incentive was offered. This need not be dramatic but should add to the urgency, being a reason, or perhaps another reason, to order *now*.
- The style of language is clearly directed at known contacts and style should always relate appropriately to the kind of people written to and the relationship that exists (or which the mailing is designed to prompt).

While these are not offered as perfect examples – I am sure there would have been a dozen other ways of going about it – they were used and they worked well. Next time, something a little different will be necessary.

Example 2. Many books

It's as difficult to find a perfect direct mail shot as it is to reproduce it in a book. The example from *The Good Book Guide* that follows is doubtless not perfect (there is no such thing), but it is good, worked well and makes a good example. *The Good Book Guide* is a publication of news and reviews about books linked to a postal ordering service. It's available on subscription (though the cost can be recouped in book orders) and is *not* a book club; there is no commitment to order.

There are two versions of the letter: a UK version and an overseas one (the UK version is shown in Figure 3.5). It's mailed with a four-colour brochure, supplementary information, order form and a reply envelope. Like many companies, the reply options now include being able to action matters via a Web site. This is a good example (and is certainly successful at drawing responses from its chosen segment), especially so because it does not promote something well known, but rather introduces and explains something and makes a persuasive case for it. Such a letter does date, and the marketing department responsible for this one reviews performance and intention regularly and continually fine-tunes the approach.

This kind of approach has a distinct flavour of what is called 'mass exclusivity', which is useful for some products/services. The phrase 'mass exclusivity', which at first sight might appear inherently contradictory, was coined to describe a promotional approach which makes what is sold, or it supplies – or both – appear exclusive, while making sure that large numbers of people see it that way. It is an approach that is enhanced by direct mail and is favoured by some who regularly promote a changing range of goods to the same customer. In the UK, catalogue promotions of companies like Rohan (idiosyncratic leisure/activity clothes) and Bibliophile (which sells discounted books in a newsletter punctuated by chatty remarks and humorous quotations) are examples of this approach.

For a small firm, which by definition will sell to a manageable number of people, this can work well. It is always worth considering

50% off the cover price of The Good
Book Guide if you reply within 14 days!

**'... if a book is worth reading, it is worth buying. No book is
worth anything... until it has been read, and re-read and loved,
and loved again.'**

John Ruskin, *Collins Dictionary of Literary Quotations*

Dear Reader

If you love good books but have trouble finding them, welcome to The Good Book Guide – the leading
worldwide book review and ordering service.

Perhaps you aren't able to get to a really good bookshop very often. And even when you can – with
100,000 new books published every year – you find the choice of titles overwhelming. So how do you
find the time or the opportunity to keep up to date with the books you want to read? And how can you
find the bookshop that carries them all in stock? How do you know which are the ones worth reading?

The Good Book Guide can help you choose and buy the best of the recently published books and
guarantees their delivery straight to your door, in any part of the world. It's a totally independent service
run by people who love books as much as you do.

Special Introductory Offer

As a special welcome to you as a new subscriber, we'd like to make you this special offer:

A FREE copy of Bill Bryson's *Mother Tongue* (worth £6.99)

A FREE copy of *The Plain English Guide* (worth £4.99)

A £5 token to put towards your first purchase

AND 50% off The Good Book Guide cover price if you reply within 14 days.

Only the best books, independently chosen and objectively reviewed

Our panel of 70 experienced reviewers reads and assesses hundreds of new hardbacks and paperbacks
every month. Only the titles they thoroughly recommend are included in the final selection – under the
careful guidance of our editorial advisers and contributors, among whom are such well-known and
respected authors as Malcolm Bradbury and Christopher Hibbert.

Unlike most other book review magazines, The Good Book Guide never accepts advertising and has no
financial ties to any publisher. We are therefore able to include books from independent and specialist
presses as well as from the larger, more established publishers. Our readers appreciate this, especially
when faced with the unwillingness of many bookshops to stock anything but current bestsellers.

One of the Guide's attractive features is that leading writers – including in recent issues Victoria
Glendinning, Jim Crace and Blake Morrison – make their own personal book selections. And putting
the boot on the other foot, established literary figures such as Robert Harris, John Mortimer and Justin
Cartwright on John Updike are also profiled.

24 Seward Street London EC1V 3GB Great Britain   Tel: +44 (0)171 490 9911 (Order Line) and +44 (0)171 490 9900 (Customer Service)
Fax: +44 (0)171 490 9908   E-mail enquiries: enquiries@good-book-guide.co.uk   E-mail orders: orders@good-book-guide.co.uk

Twelve authoritative Guides a year

As a subscriber to The Good Book Guide service, each year you will receive twelve issues of The Good Book Guide: the monthly, full-colour magazine filled with lively, concise reviews of over 300 of the most outstanding new books published.

If you're interested in the latest fiction and nonfiction, bestselling biographies, travel guides, authoritative reference works, history, art or current affairs, The Good Book Guide offers you the most stimulating and comprehensive selection of books you will find.

Straightforward service direct to your door

Once you have subscribed to the Guide, you'll not only know what is worth reading, but any book you decide to purchase will be in your hands in a matter of days.

We hold in stock all of the titles featured in the Guide, so they're ready for immediate despatch, with delivery guaranteed anywhere in the world. If you are looking for a book, video or CD-Rom that doesn't appear in the Guide, our Special Ordering Service will find it and deliver it to your door, as long as it is currently available.

Videos, CD-Roms, audios and gifts too...

In addition to the best books, we review the best releases on video – feature films, documentaries, television drama and comedy – together with the latest and best CD-Roms and audio tapes.

Through our Gift Service, you can send the perfect present to your friends and relatives anywhere in the world. Choose from an attractive range of books, videos, CD-Roms and gift ideas in the Guide and we'll gift wrap the item, enclose a personal message on a greetings card and send it to that special person.

Easy ordering – without any commitments

Once you have decided what you want to buy, the rest is easy! Simply place your order with us at any time that suits you – 24 hours a day, 365 days a year – by fax, telephone, e-mail or post.

Please note that we are NOT a book club. As a subscriber, you are under absolutely NO OBLIGATION TO PURCHASE ANYTHING from the Guide and no item will ever be sent unless you have ordered it.

And our no-quibble guarantee means that you can return anything you are not completely happy with and receive a replacement or full refund.

Your own portable Bookpoints discount

For every pound you spend you will earn one Bookpoint, giving you a credit of 5% to use on any future purchase, and this is in addition to the many special offers and discounts already available through the Guide – the more you spend, the more you save.

Why not subscribe today?

If you love reading, you can't afford to ignore The Good Book Guide. You won't find the Guide in the shops; the only way to obtain it is to take out a subscription. To take advantage of the specially reduced price, simply complete the enclosed form and return it together with your payment – £18 in the UK, £21 in Europe, £24 elsewhere – in the envelope provided and we'll do the rest.

We look forward to welcoming you to our unique service and hope to hear from you very soon.

Yours sincerely

Peter Braithwaite

Peter Braithwaite
Publisher

P.S. Don't forget – subscribe now to take advantage of our special offer worth at least £34.98. You'll receive a FREE copy of Bill Bryson's *Mother Tongue* (worth £6.99), a FREE copy of *The Plain English Guide* (worth £4.99), a £5 token and **50% off the cover price!**

Figure 3.5 An example of a UK direct mail shot

and developing an appropriate style and very often building on it consistently rather than making every new promotion completely different.

Simple... but effective

Having looked at an example, albeit a cost-effective one, which involves a number of elements: a two-page letter, enclosures, reply-paid envelope and – in the message – incentives, let us not forget how useful simple reminders may be. For example, mailing the following, with or without some incentive, samples, a trial offer coupon or whatever, can be effective:

- a postcard (used effectively by holiday companies such as hotels and travel agents – see page 51);
- a Christmas card (or other seasonal reminder);
- a copy of some other promotion (a copy to customers of a press release or the proof of a forthcoming advertisement);
- an invitation card (to an event or just using the style);
- a reminder card of a specific time (a car due to be serviced, a dental appointment);
- a message designed to fit a Filofax (or organizer/diary system);
- a card or poster designed to go on a noticeboard, perhaps mailed to a company as an offer to staff (nearby hairdresser, restaurant) or just tailored to the place (a typing service offering to produce theses at a university);
- a message on a Post-it;
- a copy of a press release;
- a testimonial;
- a label to stick on the telephone, reminding people of your number.

Some of these examples need not be posted separately; they can be distributed with the product in the way a card allowing you to request a catalogue may be slipped by a publisher into the books they sell (or, indeed, by the bookshop).

You need to keep ringing the changes. One hotel manager has kept in touch with me for almost 20 years. He has moved hotel, company and country a number of times, but about every six months something comes through the post from him. He uses a number of the simple ideas listed above – some have been repeated in different forms – but they have maintained awareness and business has resulted (otherwise I would no doubt eventually have been deleted from the list). Finally, as this example also makes clear, you need to be *systematic* and *persistent*. Building these elements into your direct mail need not be costly, and it pays dividends.

4

Sales Promotion

Added inducement to purchase

> *Throw out a sprat to catch a mackerel.*
> PROVERB

Sales promotion provides an inducement. It provides a prompt to purchase – and to purchase *now*. It does not provide the whole reason for people to buy. It is an aid to selling, not a substitute for it, and must be an ongoing part of any overall promotional programme of activity. It is not for emergency action. If there is a problem – something has to be done to boost sales, you have a clever idea – these are not, in themselves, reasons for implementing a promotional scheme. Promotions need to sit comfortably with other existing activities and be specifically designed to meet objectives you have set.

It is, however, a creative area where a good and often inexpensive idea can prove very useful; indeed some of the things that add just that extra reason to buy may be very simple yet make a real difference. There are many, many ways of adding promotion to the mix and many reasons for doing so. We will start by defining the technique further and setting out something about the various forms in which it comes, then investigate some specific ideas.

Promotional schemes may have one specific aim, or a number. These include:

- introducing new products and encouraging trial;
- attracting new customers to buy for the first time;
- maintaining attention and competitiveness through price variation;
- spreading sales and ironing out seasonal peaks and troughs;
- increasing the level of stocks (or range) held by distributors or retailers;
- prompting a greater volume to be purchased (by encouraging customers to buy ahead or extend their use of a product), or increasing frequency of use or purchase.

It operates as an inherent part of the overall activity to prompt sales and is, like other techniques, not any kind of magic formula that will make up for omissions elsewhere. This is an area where there are many different types of promotion. Not all are right for any one kind of business and the trick is to choose those that work for you and suit the kind of business you are in. To do this effectively you must focus on the customers first and foremost, asking what it is that suits them, consider the strengths and weaknesses of any range of techniques and what is most likely to bring the best results. It is also an area where it is necessary to experiment a little.

You need to try things, monitor the results and see which techniques really are best. There will not necessarily be a link between what is most 'clever' and what prompts most sales.

CATEGORIES OF PROMOTION

There are a number of ways of using sales promotion. Some of the main ones are discussed here.

In-home promotions

As the name suggests, these reach consumers in their homes, leading them direct to your place of business.

Example: the leaflets offering reduced prices that many of us receive from pizza establishments.

Other things that come through the door can include samples, coupons (redeemable for product) and linking a purchase to competitions. This can be useful if your business is in an area of manageable size and neither what is distributed, nor the cost of distributing it, need be expensive.

In-store promotions

These are promotions in retail premises (or anywhere the customers actually visit, so it could be a showroom for industrial products) and thus have the advantage that they take place where the final decision to purchase is made.

Example: the temporary price reduction is perhaps the classic example.

A large range of alternatives (some also affecting price) is also possible. These include extra value offers (economy sizes, 25 per cent free, samples banded to standard packs, etc), gifts, self-liquidating promotions (promotions that offer special price goods to be sent away for; self-liquidating because the savings made through bulk buying such gifts at a discount can cover all the costs), demonstrations and personality promotions (such as a book-signing by a famous author).

Immediate benefit promotions

The sooner the reward from any promotion is received by the customer the more likely it is to prompt them into action, so here again a temporary price reduction is a good technique; also free gifts – much used for cosmetics – and anything that gives the customer something *new*.

Example: an offer linked to the current month – wine of the month, say, in a restaurant.

Other examples of promotions directed at the ultimate consumer include trade-in allowances, other products in a range free or linked to purchase (eg buying a television gives the purchaser the right to buy a video recorder at a special price), gift vouchers (and trading stamps) and special credit terms – one that is always important in a poor economic climate.

There are dangers with all this, for while there are not necessarily high costs, there are some costs, and margins are reduced if everything is sold on a promotion-linked basis. This danger is recognized in the names certain promotional tactics are given, for example a consultant, hairdresser or anyone supplying a service may give some of their time free in the hope of selling more time as a result of whetting the customer's appetite; this is euphemistically called 'investment pricing'. It can cost a good deal and, worse, easily set precedents.

Trade promotions

Another kind of promotion is important to anyone selling down a line of distribution. If your product goes to its final customer via retailers, wholesalers, agents or distributors then they have to be persuaded to stock them and spend time and effort promoting them. How? In part it can be done by setting up promotions aimed at these people rather than at the final customer, though it should be noted that there is an appeal to these intermediaries in products that have built-in promotions for the consumer, as it makes them easier to sell. This is true even on a small scale, with someone making individual pottery items able to find more outlets to stock them if they provide those outlets with a small stand on which to display them.

Specifically such promotions may try to:

- obtain support and co-operation in stocking and promoting;
- raise stock levels and extend it across the range, thus pre-empting competitors who might otherwise take up the distributor's time and efforts.

Here are some examples of trade promotions.

Bonusing
This method, which takes the form of quantity rates to encourage ordering – '13 for the price of 12', is also used for consumers, albeit with smaller quantities – 'three for the price of two'.

Incentive schemes

These give a reward linked to the amount sold. This can be money, extra discounts, gifts or product, either for sale or for them. An example from the travel trade is where a successful travel agent selling, say, flights to the USA, will get a free trip themselves if they hit a particular target. What chance does the customer have of receiving objective advice in such circumstances? When gifts like this, rather than money, are involved, the scheme is sometimes called a 'dealer loader'.

Cooperative advertising

This can work well. It involves two (or more) parties sharing the cost of an advertisement, responses to which will benefit them both. An example of this may be a retailer and manufacturer advertising a product for sale (perhaps on special offer) at a particular store.

Provision of display material

This will encourage stocking and sale, which then encourages onward sale. Display stands have already been mentioned and there are many forms of these. Other assistance might include window stickers, posters, or any of the vast range of in-store persuasive material.

THE CREATIVE FACTOR

The tightest budget rules out some of the areas covered in this book. Advertising, for example, will produce better value for money if it is undertaken effectively, but every advertisement costs something. A major campaign may simply not be possible and though carefully chosen places for limited advertising can pay dividends, there may not be too many of these and no amount of thinking will change that fact. With promotion, however, the opposite is true. There are a great many possible ideas and thinking about what suits your business best and trying to come up with new permutations is very worth while.

Originality and creativity are two very important aspects of any successful promotion. Of course, that is not to say that there can be no copying; quite the reverse. But a creative and original scheme can, for a low budget, score points over a competitor who uses something more stereotyped, even though they spend more money on it. So, when deciding what promotion might work for you it is worth investigating what has been done by others and then making a determined effort to find, if not something entirely new, then something that contains a new slant. New or not, what is most important is that whatever is done is well suited to the company, product or service and market involved. In particular, you need to think about the kind of customer to whom you sell. What would appeal to them? How do they think? What else are they exposed to? Find something just right and real impact is possible at low cost.

The following examples illustrate not only a number of low cost ideas, but also the thinking involved in producing them. The list is not comprehensive (it never could be), but ranges across many possibilities and is designed to help stimulate the process of coming up with good ideas that suit your business. No idea will work forever; some are in any case topical in some way and it is necessary over time to ring the changes. Those listed provide examples of various sorts, illustrate the range of possibilities and can doubtless be adapted to provide still more ideas. The ways in which they work are not mutually exclusive, as ideas overlap, sometimes using the same approach in different ways, so the headings are not intended to convey that other ideas have none of the essence of the particular description. Thus, the first example is certainly memorable in the literal sense, but so are others. Indeed, if people are to remember you there must be something of this in every idea.

Making it memorable

Sometimes all that is necessary to create something that produces ongoing promotional impact is one simple but novel idea. One small hotel in Gloucestershire came up with the idea of having a teddy bear on every bed and a floating duck in every bathroom. It is a touch people are highly likely to remember. It can be linked to other items of promotion, such as brochures, and even creates an additional sales opportunity. Customers can buy a bear or duck to take home – and they regularly do so.

It never rains, but...

Another idea that will be remembered and is also useful to people is used by an English coffee shop, taking advantage of the country's predictably uncertain climate. They have hit on the idea of renting umbrellas. You pay a deposit, use the brolly to get yourself home without getting wet and return it another day (getting back your deposit). A good deal of extra business comes from people making the return visit or simply waiting a while 'to see if the rain eases off' before deciding to hire. This has another useful characteristic – it can easily become a habit for local customers.

Only for you

Sometimes an idea can usefully be directed at groups other than customers. One firm, selling direct to other businesses, constructed a promotion (a chance to win a holiday if you ordered regularly) for the secretaries of their buyers. The secretaries often made the decisions unilaterally on behalf of their bosses, so this worked well – messages were even sent in part in shorthand to give a feeling of exclusivity, as only the secretary could read them.

Something to catch the eye

Many shops have 'island' display units on which products are displayed on all sides and positioned so that customers can walk right round them. In a few shops I have seen such units on wheels and these are regularly rotated to give customers a different view. This is especially useful near the entrance, since by making the shop look a little different more people, pausing at the door and thinking 'Shall I go in?' are likely to enter and browse – and then buy.

Advance news

Interest is maintained in some shops by posting news of forthcoming developments (soon to be released videos in a video hire shop or soon to be published books in a book shop, displaying covers, perhaps). Any business can use the trick of telling customers something twice: once when it is about to happen, again when it does.

Free trial

Giving something away – a sample – works well if it encourages first and then subsequent purchases. Do not simply make it an option: ask specifically or send it unbidden. A company from whom I buy office stationery sent me a sample of a correcting fluid recently. It really seemed better than the brand we had used previously and I ordered more, something I would never have done without trying it.

This is, unsurprisingly, an important area. Everyone likes something for nothing. Sometimes there are possibilities of making an offer significant to the decision to buy, yet not to the volume of business to be obtained. Another example shows this in action: a travel agent after business travel accounts with companies might offer a reduction to staff of the firm booking holidays with them, or a free holiday each year for the managing directors (or whoever appoints the agent). Either method is a small price to pay for the volume of business travel involved.

A word from our sponsor

Sponsorship tends to conjure up images of big business, signs at major sporting events and concerts at the Barbican. But it can be much simpler. An instant print company supplies cafés around the town where they operate with ashtrays, and as you sit and eat or drink there is ample time to take down their phone number. My firm of accountants sponsors a local amateur theatrical society, a good one, and uses the first nights and other functions to entertain its local clients. Look at your own situation for such links, since there are certainly low cost opportunities and there may well be ones that suit you.

Who were those people?

Don't kid yourself that even past (and satisfied) customers will be so dazzled by your excellence that they will remember you forever.

People's recall is strictly limited, and they may have more important things to do than remember or make a note of your telephone number. Give them something to make it easy. Christmas is the classic gift time. A bottle of Scotch may be nice, but after it is received it is soon gone. A permanent reminder may be money better spent. Pens and desk items, especially good ones (not necessarily the most expensive) are likely to be kept and will be there in front of the recipient whenever they say: 'Who were those people?'

Keep them coming back

Any scheme that links one purchase to another does this, or at least encourages the process. Loyalty schemes for regular customers are an example and the advantage need not be money. For instance, a wine merchant can offer quantity discounts to keep customers coming back, but might also use wine tastings. Coupons linked to the next purchase are also a common form.

You can afford it

Credit is important. Customers find it attractive, but remember it costs you money and should not be given away lightly. If you consider the simple procedure of giving customers more time to pay – one month more, say – then you must work out the cost very clearly and bear in mind that these days some people will abuse almost any terms you may agree with them. Formal credit schemes and making hire purchase or leasing schemes easier and more attractive work well in certain businesses.

We can make it easy

Some purchases are complex and recognized as such by many customers. For every person who knows all about computers, for example, there are no doubt several who are very wary. Do you buy the cheapest or the surest? Good advice makes a good promotion. This can take the form of an event (see Chapter 5) or individual counselling. Many technical companies successfully use advice and the promise of expert and understandable help as a promotional offer.

Guaranteed!

Special guarantees can be offered, in other words something a little better than expected or the industry norm. This is a classic 'me too' area and it may be hard to keep ahead. Just look how car manufacturers offer longer and longer warranty periods and associated benefits.

Here's how

If using the product demands any kind of skill, then training can become an effective promotion. This may be partial, as with a reduction in the cost of a typing course with a typewriter purchase (or just a how-to-do-it book), or complete – a course to show you exactly how to operate a photocopier, for instance.

In the bag

The container can become a plus and an incentive to purchase for some things. A small honey producer selling the product in a jar nice enough to keep and reuse found sales increased despite a higher price, especially to those wanting to give the product as a present. (Incidentally, finding out why purchases happen may be an excellent stimulus to promotional ideas, and present giving is a case in point.)

The right time

The simplest example of a promotion that revolves around time is perhaps the 'happy hour'. Here the bar sells drinks at a reduced price (or on a basis such as two for one) and the time is judged carefully to fill the establishment at an otherwise low time or to encourage people to stay on after the happy hour is over. Many promotions can be structured around timing: weekend breaks in a hotel, seasonal sales, last chance to buy at an existing price, special deal when first open, etc. The timings in your own business – slack periods, seasonal variations, etc – will probably give you some ideas here.

Win a prize

Competitions need not be expensive to organize. Someone selling children's toys or clothes might link a promotion to, say, a painting competition. The value is in how this competition can be linked to a number of communications. The announcement, the judging and the prize all afford PR opportunities beyond the basic event.

Incidentally, prizes can often be organized on a swap basis with other non-competitive organizations. For example, a travel agent and a fashion shop might swap a weekend break and a new outfit. Often suppliers may be prepared to provide their product or service at a reduced rate if the scheme will bring them publicity.

'Wow!', 'Arh!' and 'Whatever next?'

Promotion can have a role in drawing attention that has frankly very little to do with the product or service and which may be considered silly. Such impact may still be useful, as these examples show:

- *Signpost.* A barrage balloon moored above the site of a business may be a good way of reminding the public of its opening (or of a special occasion like a sale) but is not for every day, nor would it work without other advertising as it would not be clear what its purpose was.
- A *nice touch*. A gift can act as a reminder and be nice to receive without being of any real monetary value. For example, the things given out if you fly business class, such as sleep masks, are not only useful on the flight but are often retained afterwards and act as a reminder. A similar example is the single orchid given to all passengers on Thai Airways.
- A *lesson*. This may prove irresistible to some. One computer outlet offered juggling lessons in the shopping precinct outside its office, hiring someone to do it and creating quite a stir as people queued to have a go. The link to the product was tenuous, but the impact was there.

PROMOTION METHODOLOGY

Promotion offers some reason, often a reason additional to the excellence of the product, for buying. It does not form an exclusive methodology. In other words, a good promotional idea can be put over and communicated in many different ways, for example:

- in an advertisement;
- via direct mail (including the simplest forms of reminder cards etc);
- in newsletters;
- signs (eg window stickers in a shop).

Indeed a current promotion can colour everything for a while, by being mentioned in sales letters, on the telephone and – like the hotel teddy bears mentioned earlier – by just being visible. On many occasions the best way to put over a promotional scheme will be through a combination of methods. A number of elements, well orchestrated, can provide the best impact, for it is less a question of asking which one method is best, rather of seeing how each can play its role in achieving the overall effect.

With the sheer volume of ideas that can be used to create an appropriate promotion, plus the range of methods of putting it over, there is a need for a systematic approach: suggestions as to the thinking that will generate this are reviewed below.

The only thing that characterizes successful sales promotion schemes is that they work. Some of the seemingly most appropriate can go badly wrong, as Hoover's ill-fated offer of free flights did, resulting in more bad publicity than they surely intended when many found the arrangements were not as straightforward as they felt they should have been. Even though this is now a few years ago, it is widely remembered. Other schemes can be clever but impracticable. I remember a colleague of mine suggesting once some years ago that the ultimate promotional offer was to give a budgerigar with every packet of birdseed. The economics made sense, but the animal protection organizations would – at the very least – have felt it worthy of some comment! The idea never saw the light of day. A checklist style summary of the way to create successful promotions follows.

Getting the best out of promotion

Promotion is very much an ideas area and as such it is easy to be carried away by your enthusiasm for a particular plan, so much so that you may not implement it in the best possible way. Because of this it is worth following some systematic guidelines, thus:

1. *Decide clear objectives.* While there are many different results a promotional scheme may achieve, they cannot do everything at once. Be clear what you are really trying to do with a promotion and make sure the way it is organized is lined up behind firm objectives.
2. *Consider all the options.* There is a wide range of ways of organizing promotion. One idea may seem appropriate, but it is always worth reviewing alternatives – or amendments – to any particular scheme to check there is not another, better, way to meet the objectives.
3. *Make it novel.* This is not always essential, as some 'me too' promotions and simple ideas may suit you well. However, if a creative approach can be found then you may succeed in creating greater impact – and sales – for the same input of time and money.
4. *Test first.* Again the enthusiasm for a creative idea may lead to skipping this stage, but many ideas can be tested on a limited basis initially and this may save money by, for example, allowing revisions to be made before the scheme is extended.
5. *Regard promotion as an important part of the mix.* Promotion may well need some thought, organization and setting up. Compared with, say, repeating a simple advertisement in a trade journal, it may seem the more complicated option. It suits those on a tight budget well, there is an almost infinite number of ideas, and this technique of bringing in the business deserves its fair share of time, maybe more.
6. *Ring the changes.* Again, this is not an irrevocable rule (some good, simple schemes can go on and on and remain effective), but it is worth seeking new ideas and new slants on old ones to keep the whole approach fresh. Before any promotion can act to persuade people to buy, it must be noticed; something new is more likely to do this.
7. *A final guideline.* Do not expect promotion, however good, to prop up or get over other weaknesses. If distribution, display or the product itself have weaknesses then no promotion, however

novel, will make up for it, and in the long term such problems must be sorted out.

A plethora of possibilities

Other ideas are perennial. Providing a Santa Claus for children to visit in a department store at Christmas is a seasonal promotion that links logically with Christmas shopping and looks set to go on forever. Some seem to follow fashion: an idea is used somewhere and suddenly it is everywhere. Once you could not buy petrol in the UK without being given some form of drinking glass or the coupons to collect them. More recently, weekend breaks and other incentives linked to hotels seem to be everywhere; and tomorrow it will be something else. Some ideas are worth copying (or better still amending), but avoid being at the end of a trend or a season; you will get no extra business linking your promotion to beach balls once the holiday season is over and nothing is so dead as a forgotten craze.

Finally, in this area, remember that you are not after one magic promotion that will change your business permanently, rather a number of things, ringing the changes to refocus attention and making sure that customers see them as appropriate (would you go to the doctor who gave a free pair of roller skates to every patient whose leg he set?) and that you merge them in suitably with the rest of your communications strategy. No one can rely on being remembered for ever even by their best customers, nor will you attract new customers simply by the excellence of your product or service. The competition may well offer something they say is just as good.

You need to keep on reminding customers and potential customers that you are there, giving them a reason to buy from you rather than from others – and a reason for buying now rather than later. Promotion can help with all of this, provided it is thought out and tailored to the business objectives involved. Don't let what seems like a good idea run away with you before thinking it through (a process which often shows something to be neither irresistible nor clever), but don't neglect thinking up new angles either. If you're finding it difficult to come up with the right ideas this doesn't mean your competitors are in the same boat. The scope here is enormous. Sales promotion ranges from the simplest and most low cost methods to grand and expensive schemes; there may be ideas you can use at either end of the spectrum, or somewhere inbetween.

5

Making an Exhibition of Yourself

Getting the most from exhibitions and trade fairs

It is easy to be wise after the event.
PROVERB

Exhibitions are hard work. Not least they are hard on the feet and sometimes the stomach. This may well be as true of those who visit them as those who organize and exhibit at them. Nevertheless, many take place and many people make use of them – indeed, I met the publishers of this book at an exhibition, so they can certainly produce results.

If you are on a very tight budget then major exhibitions may well be ruled out, though some people get round this with a shared stand, working with others who are non-competitive. But the range of events coming under the exhibition heading is substantial and includes many smaller – and local – events, from country shows and fairs to events put on by local chambers of trade. Even a village fête may be an opportunity for a small stand, and I know of one company selling dried flower arrangements for which the latter is a regularly successful activity. What matters is not simply the overall cost, which is always important, but more the cost per enquiry or per order. This may well be an area where you need to seek opportunities to experiment to see how cost-effectively it could work for your business.

You must look at every exhibition possibility in a very hard-nosed way. Exhibition organizers will always tend to say their show is right for you (for everyone?), indeed those selling exhibition space can be somewhat 'pushy'. Each possible event needs checking out. If you do decide to participate, what you get from it will be in direct proportion to the way in which you undertake it. So here we review the principles of successful exhibiting. These involve factors that are perhaps best described as promotional, but they also overlap into selling techniques, which are discussed in Chapter 6.

Exhibitions produce a unique environment. And there are a lot of them (the Exhibition Industry Federation describes it as an industry worth some £2 billion); because of the scale, a good deal of research exists about exhibitions, as follows:

■ Attendees are, they say, receptive to what exhibitors have to sell. They have given up time to check out specific areas and there are none of the usual distractions of the office, phones, interruptions, etc while they do so.

■ The cost of a lead generated at an exhibition is low (certainly compared to sales people's time) and they require, on average, less follow-up contact to convert.

■ They provide a quality audience. The great majority of visitors have buying influence, more than half are middle management and above. Special categories are useful too; for example, a third of those visiting exhibitions are new to their job, needing to check things out fast and actively looking for new suppliers.

■ The average visitor spends five hours at an exhibition and, in addition to seeking new contacts, spends much of the time talking to people he or she knows (so it is a good way of maintaining contact with existing customers).

In addition, exhibitions are, of course, interactive. Products can be touched and tried and demonstrations watched; feedback is immediately available and progress towards a decision can be certain and fast. Further, many exhibitions are specialist; in fact, the fastest growing sector is that where exhibitors are all from one industry.

DANGERS AND OPPORTUNITIES

Of course there are dangers and it is certainly possible to exhibit for the wrong reasons – because competitors are there; because customers expect it; to entertain. But there are also opportunities and there are certainly many good reasons for exhibiting. These need not be mutually exclusive, but should be thought through if everything is to be considered and the arrangements made to achieve everything we want. You may want, for example:

- to take direct orders on the stand;
- to demonstrate something;
- to provide information (and get information about competitors);
- to find names/contacts for long-term conversion;
- to meet/entertain agents or distributors;
- to achieve public relations and press coverage;
- to introduce or test a new product or promotion;
- to do some market research.

Whatever the reasons, they should be reviewed and agreed *before* the event. Some may be incompatible; for instance, sales people will have less time to take orders if they are completing lengthy research questionnaires with prospects. All the objectives need to be specifically reflected in the organization and arrangements.

You also need to have clear *sales objectives*. These may not always be simply to take orders, but can also usefully include:

- arranging a trial;
- arranging a demonstration at their premises or yours;
- agreeing/arranging a further meeting;
- discussing details to allow a quotation/proposal/survey to follow.

Exhibitions are people-intensive and you need to establish who should attend and take part – sales, service, technical, export, management and so on; and also who will remain to 'mind the shop'.

Setting clear objectives is the first task when considering taking part in an exhibition. With these objectives in mind preparations can commence in earnest.

PREPARATION

This must be systematic and thorough. There will be 101 details to check, from the product samples you want to take to making sure you pack the coffee mugs (remember nothing or virtually nothing will be provided by the organizer). I asked Susan Cline of Design Consultancy Services in London, who has much experience in this area, how preparation should be approached. She quoted three key preliminary areas:

1. *Assess the exhibition.* Will it attract the type of visitor who could become your client? Will some of your existing clients go there? Will there be enough visitors to make it worth your while? What about the exhibitors? They are as important as the visitors. A company is known by the company it keeps. How many exhibitors will there be? What kind of companies will be represented? Will your closest competitors and rivals be there? Is so, can you afford not to show your face?
2. *Assess the timing.* The timing of the show is very important. Will you have suitable staff who can devote time to being on the stand? Watch out for conflicting commitments such as delivery or production dates.
3. *Assess the cost.* The rent for the stand and the cost of having it constructed and dressed are only the most obvious elements. There are other expenses to take into account. Remember to include the cost of travel, food and accommodation for staff, also the cost of drinks and hospitality for clients at the exhibition.

WHAT MUST YOU DO ONCE YOU'VE DECIDED TO TAKE A STAND?

First, build up a good relationship with the organizer. Have a named contact for them to work with. Make sure that they know what you need and that everyone in your company also knows what is required; the company must speak with one voice.

Through that contact make sure that the position of your stand is suitable. Is it within a group of similar services or merchandise and not isolated among unrelated stands? It may be possible to negotiate a better position (or even a better deal) with the organizer if you have taken trouble from the start to establish a good working relationship.

Find out from the organizers what services they supply to exhibitors for each stand. For example, will they arrange for lighting and furniture to be supplied as part of the basic package, or will that involve extra expense? Certainly you need to check carefully what will be needed – everything from chairs to literature displays – and make sure it will be available in suitable form on the day. What opportunities are there for free publicity or linked publicity as part of the overall exhibition arrangements?

You don't want all visitors to be chance ones. It is an opportunity to meet with existing customers, to catch up with dormant ones and for contact with others you have yet to persuade to spare time for real discussions. Such people need to be invited to attend.

Presentation on the day is of the utmost importance. You must communicate a clear and simple message. Make sure that the image presented by the stand represents your company, as you would want it to be. Make it welcoming. Do not create any barrier that might seem daunting for a visitor to cross – no physical barrier, no design barrier and no psychological barrier. It can be helpful to have something of particular interest near the front of the stand. Then visitors can approach it without feeling that they are encroaching on to your territory and without worrying that some over-zealous sales person will pounce on them. All this needs preplanning.

Staff briefing, and perhaps training, for exhibition work are essential. Everyone who serves on the stand must appear competent, alert and interested. Make sure well before the event that they each have a job to do and targets to aim for.

All this and more must be geared to the overall effect that the stand seeks to have. The key intention should not be simply to be visible (however smart or professional that visibility is), but to make that visibility link to a truly persuasive presence.

MAKING YOUR PRESENCE PERSUASIVE

The stand is not simply a static advertisement. The whole point of exhibiting is to meet people; they need to be encouraged on to the stand and persuaded towards your objectives. Consider some of the many reasons why people visit exhibitions. They not only come to do business and place orders, but also to:

- set up a future appointment;
- see a demonstration;
- deal with specific technical queries;
- negotiate the best terms;
- see new products/ideas;
- find answers to a problem;
- take a decision to purchase;
- compare the range of competitors;
- collect information for the future;
- test/try products.

All these need handling in different ways and may mean deploying a range of differing skills. The person who runs the best demonstrations, for instance, may not be the best negotiator.

Others may visit your stand. These include your competitors, professional literature collectors, drink scroungers and other time-wasters. You also may be visited by some disgruntled customers – they come with a complaint or to moan about discounts; things you would prefer not to deal with publicly at an exhibition. The good exhibitor can spot such people at 20 paces, indeed doing so is an ability that should be cultivated.

You must also cultivate the ability to handle people in this strange environment. An exhibition provides a rare opportunity for customers to talk to three potential suppliers in the same hour; they take full advantage of this, but they do also regard it as a 'day out'. They expect to be treated well and all expect you to deal with them individually as if they were the only visitor to the exhibition, or at least to your stand. It may be the only time they meet you on 'your patch' and the encounter must make a lasting and positive impression. For those who know you less well (or not at all), you must create a welcoming front and not let them find the show, or your stand in particular, daunting.

Persuasive techniques must be used at every stage of the contact. The techniques of making face-to-face meetings persuasive are reviewed, in detail, in Chapter 6, which you may find worth reading in conjunction with this chapter. Here we look at a number of issues that are specific to the exhibition scene.

The first step is to encourage those moving through the exhibition to come on to your stand. People can be actively put off by both the stand and those staffing it. So avoid:

- obstructing gangways/entrances;
- the sales people lining up and appearing as a barrier;
- staff gathering in groups, talking together;
- leaving parts of the stand unattended;
- any clutter with files, bags, coats, used coffee cups, untidy tables, full ashtrays etc;
- the cosy, 'do not disturb' look, with staff sitting around on all the available seats;
- people looking bored, aggressive, defensive, tired;
- staff being *too* eager to get someone on to the stand;
- high pressure 'pointing'.

Make sure that the stand is clean, accessible, open, well lit, interesting, neither too crowded nor too empty and has clear spaces, an element of movement, something going on (a video, a demonstration), a clear enquiry point, literature available – and accessible, smart, welcoming staff (identified by badges or uniforms). It is key that visitors can easily:

- see the product;
- read displays (you should check type sizes);
- find and take literature;
- watch anything going on;
- ask questions;
- prompt more detailed discussions.

Everything about the set-up must make it easy and welcoming for visitors to come on to the stand; every detail counts.

ESTABLISHING CONTACT

Not saying 'Can I help you?'

Nobody, but nobody, should _ever_ say 'Can I help you?' (to which most say, instinctively, 'No thank you'). Everyone on the stand needs to be prepared to take a positive and appropriate initiative. It is just as off-putting as 'Can I help you?' to have a sales person launch into a long and technical explanation replete with jargon. If you start with a question, it must be an _open_ question, in other words, something that doesn't lend itself to being answered by 'Yes' or 'No' (this is the main problem with the hackneyed 'Can I help you?'). Something that demands a fuller reply tends to do better; for instance:

> 'What are you hoping to find at the show?'
> 'How much do you know about us?'
> 'Where are you from?'

Equally, don't frighten people off. There are probably people jumping out at them every few yards, so remember the purpose of this first contact is to:

- make the visitor feel at ease;
- get them talking;
- discover their exact interest;
- identify their needs;
- get them deciding it's _worth_ spending some time with you.

So, try to start with unchallenging openings:

- introduce yourself by name (this can often result in the visitor giving you his or her name in return);
- offer a quick demonstration or video explanation of the point attracting attention;
- discuss the visitor's particular point of interest or need;
- ask general questions to open the conversation, such as, 'What do you use (product) for?', 'When might you be considering upgrading?', continuing to favour open questions as you do so.

The overall aim is to move effortlessly into a relaxed and interesting conversation, not to 'hassle' people.

Once such a conversation is under way the next key stage is the better identification of individual needs. At this point the approach must be tailored towards the kind of person who has come on to the stand – an existing or dormant customer, a prospect, someone 'just looking', a competitor – with more specific questions leading the way (see Chapter 6 for more details).

Not everyone will be worth time and attention, but once you establish that someone is not a real prospect, always handle them politely and professionally (remember, they may be a future customer, or will know a potential customer, or be useful in some other way). If they require information or assistance, give it to them quickly and politely, but do not waste time if the stand is busy. If the stand is quiet, a 'just looking' visitor can be valuable – a stand with people already on it and talking tends to encourage others to stop and look.

Remember also that not everyone has the inclination, or the time, to talk to you on the day. But they are presumably involved in the topic of the event and you may want to follow them up either specifically and individually or, at the least, add them to a mailing list. So, one of the prime jobs at exhibitions is to collect names, but how do you get these names? The classic way is to have a goldfish-type bowl for people to drop business cards into, though you may need to give them a reason to do so. A draw, with a prize, often in the form of product (which is cheapest) seems to work well. Do think about prizes, however. A bottle of champagne may be nice, but is a bit hackneyed, and yet, unless you are a travel agent, a fortnight in the Bahamas is costly to provide. Swapping products works well. Team up with another (non-competitive) exhibitor and let them give something you provide as a prize and vice versa; this will make both stands look more creative. Anything that can be added to this sort of technique to get more from it should be built in:

- run a draw every day (not just at the end of the exhibition);
- announce the time of the draw;
- make it an 'event', eg get someone well known to do it;
- announce the winner(s) (in a press release, notice, etc);
- if the prize is an 'event' (eg a flight in a hot air balloon) report on it later and follow it up by keeping in touch with the winner(s).

If cost is a big factor it may be better to have one memorable, noticeable, prize rather than several routine ones.

Finally, keep an eye on those depositing cards. I once saw one exhibition visitor depositing a whole box of cards in the bowl in an attempt to raise the odds of winning an attractive prize. Besides, some are deposited at just the right moment to engage them in conversation.

AFTER THE BALL IS OVER

One of the most crucial areas of exhibiting happens after the event, and that is follow-up action. Too often people visit a stand, express interest, leave a business card, are promised a later contact – but never hear another word (or hear so long afterwards that it only produces a negative reaction). This negates all the effort – time and money – that has gone into being there and is neither good public relations nor good selling.

It must _always_ be the case that every encounter on the stand prompts certain specific actions, so whoever meets the customer must remember:

- to give their business card to every visitor;
- that every visitor's name, company, address and telephone number should be recorded;*
- that outline details of the enquiry should be noted;*
- that action must be highlighted and implemented as promised;
- that if action is to be taken by someone not present at the show, details must be passed on;*
- that if there is any delay, an acknowledgement letter should be sent to the customer (these should be ready _before_ the event, at least in outline – they may need personalizing).

*A tailor-made form may be useful for all these points.

Not only should such information be used to prompt and record further action – it may, after all, take several contacts or a number of meetings to tie down firm business – but it should be used to analyse the results in the longer term. How many leads were there? How many were converted to business? After how long? (And at what cost?) What other contacts were made? Were any public relations activities possible – and useful? These and other questions need asking and answering.

Hopefully, there will be a general sense of euphoria after the exhibition. It went well. The stand didn't fall down. We didn't exceed the drinks budget. And there were many visitors, all expressing interest and pleasure at seeing us. Such a feeling must be borne out by the facts. With a tight budget you have to decide whether this may, or may not, be an exhibition to attend in future. The record of achievement will help plan future actions.

So, what – specifically – should you analyse? It will depend on the type of business you are in. It should include internal and external factors and is worth thinking through to produce a comprehensive list that suits you. The following will help prompt the necessary thinking:

- How many prospect names were collected?
- How many orders were taken?
- How many specific enquiries received? (Or requests for quotes or any other interim stage?)
- How many follow-up meetings were fixed?
- How much actual business (orders) was done?
- How well were the objectives achieved?
- How well did all the arrangements go?
- And, of course, what thoughts do you have about what to do differently next time?

This post-exhibition analysis can be very useful. Preparing for and running the exhibition will have been a busy period. Immediately afterwards, with follow-up activity to implement and everything that has been going on 'back at the ranch' to catch up on, it is all too easy to neglect this analysis. A series of exhibitions that build on the experience of past ones will be much more valuable in the long term.

Finally, a reminder: don't reject this area out of hand as being too expensive. Exhibiting is a prime method of contacting large numbers of people in a short period of time. If it suits you it can be a very valuable technique. It is worth a systematic review of what is available in your area (geographically or otherwise). Check your local:

- press (including business publications);
- Chambers of Commerce or trade; and
- societies (including local branches of national bodies).

Keep your eyes open for anything that might give you a platform. Do this regularly and you might be surprised at the opportunities you spot. Large or small, the next step, as we have seen, is to go about exploiting them in a thorough and professional way; then the returns can very well prove cost-effective.

6

Face-to-face Persuasion

The gentle art of salesmanship

We are all salesmen every day of our lives.
CHARLES M SCHWAB

Everybody sells something, it is said, but many people avoid selling or do it ineffectively. Selling has a poor image; it can conjure up pictures of the hard-selling encyclopaedia salesman with his foot in the door and his hand in your wallet before you can say even the first word of 'Not today, thank you.' This is a pity, because selling is no more than helping people to buy. It need not upset customers, indeed it must not if you want them to feel the approach is acceptable and come back for more. But it must be persuasive. There is more to it than having the 'gift of the gab' and 'born sales people', if any exist, are too thin on the ground to rely on your being one, or your finding one easily to bring into the business. Sales effectiveness comes from an awareness of the processes involved and a careful deployment of the techniques in an individually tailored way. It involves the right approach, customer by customer, meeting by meeting, day by day.

Having said that, even the most simple application of sales-manship can pay dividends. All of the following can rightly be called 'selling' or make a useful step in that direction:

- Approaching someone in a store (or at an exhibition) and saying 'May I help you?' Better still if this stock question can be varied: 'What kind of thing are you looking for?'
- The one word shouted by the street seller of newspapers: *'Standard! Standard!'*
- The waiter who says, 'Dessert, Sir?' Better still if he brings the sweet trolley first so that you *see* how tempting they are (this is merchandising as well as selling).
- The barman who asks, 'Another drink?' or 'A large one?'
- The aircrew with their trolley saying, 'Duty free?'
- The market stall owner selling on price: '40p a pound to you and if you can buy 'em cheaper I'll eat my hat.'

In other words, just a phrase, a question, even one word can begin the process and, in some cases, it *is* the process. All demand taking the initiative and may well prompt thoughts of similar circumstances in your business which can be approached this way, and this simply.

Also potentially powerful and absurdly simple is what has become known as the 'gin and tonic' technique. This comes from the retailer who, asked for a bottle of gin, says as he places it on the counter, 'And how many mixers would you like?' It can seem no more than a polite suggestion, but it sells the range. Such possibilities are almost endless: cigarettes and matches, nuts and bolts, strawberries and cream, computers and software, pen and paper, shoes and shoe polish. The products can be large or small, more or less expensive, with the more expensive either the main purchase or the additional suggestion.

Using such techniques, if that is not too grand a word, needs only a recognition of the possibilities and the active cultivation of a habit in yourself and any others in an appropriate position. As such they certainly qualify as low cost. Salespeople, on the other hand, are an expensive resource: they need a salary (and often commission), a car and all the associated costs of a mobile employee. But the difference between effective selling and less effective selling is not necessarily costly. Many people in the business may need to understand and practise the rudiments of selling and the better they can tackle it the more cost-effective it will be.

This chapter will now concentrate principally on techniques, though there are some implementation ideas along the way. We start with some low cost ways of finding someone to sell to, then review something of the sales techniques that can make customer contact persuasive, and end with a word about the link between sales and service and ways of stealing a march on more faint-hearted rivals.

LOW COST PROSPECTING

'Cold calling' is normally no one's favourite sales activity, and sitting down to comb through the *Yellow Pages* is both soul-destroying and such a broad-brush approach that it is never going to produce very substantial results. Yet many businesses need a regular supply of new prospects, and these have to be found; it should be an active process. It is made easier and more cost-effective by using a regular and systematic approach:

> *Rule 1*. Set time aside on a regular basis and set yourself targets. 'Every Thursday I will spend two hours prospecting' or, 'Every week I will make 10 (or 20) new contacts.'
> *Rule 2*. Put in train a number of prospect-generating mechanisms which mean you will create a regular supply of names to contact (however you do this, by telephone or by letter).

In other words, use habit to help ensure the appropriate activity occurs. The following ideas are illustrative of the approach in Rule 2, but you may well be able to think of more.

Ten prospecting methods

1. Endless chain

This, as the name suggests, is simply using one prospect to lead to another. A first may come, let's say, as an enquiry. Once we know who they are, what they might be interested in, why they came to us – in other words as we begin to know something about them – then we can ask to whom they, in turn, can direct us. This may be in two ways:

1. Asking them: 'Do you know anyone else who might be interested... ?'
2. Analysis: 'If this bank manager is interested, which others can I talk to?'

2. Centres of influence

These are people or organizations through whom you may make contact with numbers of prospects on a regular basis, because they have the power to introduce or recommend.

They may include trade and professional bodies, Chambers of Commerce, associations, banks and others. It is worth thinking through which may be useful in your business, listing them and systematically keeping in touch to ensure they know of you, they know something about what you do and are reminded of this and kept up to date. (Share with your colleagues the task of keeping in touch, each taking responsibility for a number of such contacts.) Any contact that can lead to numbers of new customers is likely to be both worth while and cost-effective if contact is maintained systematically.

3. Personal observation

This should never be underestimated. If you develop the habit of being observant, a regular supply of new prospects can follow. First, consider things in print. You need to review regularly any journals, newspapers or publications of relevance to your business. Trade or industry journals are a good example. So are in-house newsletters if you have major companies as customers who produce them and, yes, they will often put you on the list – provided you ask. News of companies, developments, staff changes, relocations and more can all provide information to lead you to a new prospect. The Internet provides a new source of such information.

Secondly, keep your eyes open and check anything that might help you. Ask yourself who has moved into the new office block on the corner or into the office next door to someone you already visit. Again, such observation (and perhaps a little associated research) can lead to new names and thus new prospects.

4. Chance contacts

This is closely related to personal observation, but worth a separate mention. I have twice obtained work following a conversation with someone sitting next to me on an aeroplane, when idle chatter – 'How much did you pay for your ticket?' and if it was cheaper than yours, 'Where did you buy it?' – identified common business interests. And once I even got work from someone whose office I wandered into, lost, to seek directions in the maze of corridors of an office block.

Beware, of course, of taking this too far, but keep an eye open for such opportunities, particularly in places where people of similar interests meet – a trade association meeting, perhaps.

5. 'Cold canvass'

Simply knocking on doors is probably not to be recommended to anyone but the bravest. However, one variant may well be useful. In places where different businesses exist close by each other, such as on an industrial estate or in an office block, it may be worth knocking on some doors near to an existing visit; not to try to sell them something, but to discover names for subsequent follow up (perhaps by telephone). Ask the receptionist who is in charge of buying office stationery, travel or whatever. Again, even a few new names may be useful and they will be geographically convenient too, which aids productivity if you subsequently need to visit them regularly.

6. Lists

By lists, I mean not so much the big ones like *Yellow Pages*, but the small, specialist ones. Association membership lists, interest groups, sports clubs; whatever ties in with your business area. This can yield names for small mailings and can be made manageable by being reviewed progressively with mailings following at so many per week. Some research on what lists exist is often well worth while.

7. Past clients/contacts

Although if you are systematic there should be few of these, there will be some. People may have good reasons for stopping doing business with you, some of which have nothing to do with you: someone leaves the company, a budget is cut, expenditure is delayed – there are many reasons. If so, always check for when things may change again, note it in the diary, however far ahead, and remember to get in touch and keep in touch as appropriate during any enforced gap. Of course, if you have *not* been very systematic in the past, it may well be worth a comprehensive search of the 'archives'.

Remember, a customer for one product in your range, but not for another, may be persuaded to buy both. One hotel discovered it could boost its restaurant trade by mailing its meetings business clients, who were recorded in a separate file and had previously been neglected.

8. Suppliers

Anyone with whom you do business might be persuaded to do business with you if your product or service is something they buy. You know them. They know you. They doubtless want to retain your business, so they are unlikely to reject out of hand a suggestion to talk.

Further, you will no doubt have a good record of such people in your accounts department and need to do little more than check through the invoices they send you to identify them.

9. Extracurricular activities

Business and pleasure do not always mix, but sometimes they do. A good number of business deals are struck on the golf course, just as legend would have it. It may be worth reviewing what you do, where you go, what clubs or associations you belong to, and seeing whether you can get more from them in a business sense. This is definitely an area to approach with care; after all the membership committee may not approve (though if you were on the committee maybe you would make more contacts).

10. Directories

There are so many directories published that, certainly in the UK, there is a directory of directories – *Current British Directories*. This implies there could well be one or more that you don't currently know about that could be useful to you. Check it out; even one with some good new names can be useful.

A word that has fairly recently come into use is 'networking'. Some would define this as a combination of several of the above – it could include centres of influence, extracurricular activities and other contacts – but a key element of true networking is collaboration, in other words a network of people seeking similar, but preferably uncompetitive, business. They keep in touch and work together to produce and swap leads. Certainly this happens in consultancy. For example, one of those I keep in touch with is an expert on market research (an area in which I need some support), and I've quoted him in Chapter 1. Like all the above, this is worth exploring. There can, of course, be some costs, but these need not be great and some, like commission paid around a network, are incurred only after business has resulted for you.

Having found names to contact, the next step may be to set up appointments with them. The kind of telephone call this necessitates is dealt with in Chapter 8, which discusses telephone selling in its various forms. Beyond that, the next step is to make sure any meeting you or your colleagues have with them is genuinely persuasive; that is, it uses appropriate sales techniques.

TECHNIQUES TO MAKE YOUR APPROACH PERSUASIVE

There is a good deal to this subject (I have written at length on it in *101 Ways to Increase Your Sales*) and even devoting the major part of a chapter to it necessitates being selective. But it is important. In many small businesses the principals do not have a sales background, as their prime expertise may be something quite different – the engineering on which the product is based perhaps. But, while selling may not be your stock in trade, or even your favourite part of the business process, it must be done and done well.

Selling, to repeat the earlier definition, is helping people to buy. You cannot sell without understanding how and why people buy. In a small company where many will have outside contact with people who are at some stage of the buying process, this understanding of buying is very important. By understanding the buying process and seeing its connection with selling you can see that magical talents are not needed in order to be a satisfactory seller.

The process of selling cannot take place without communication, and that requires two people: the buyer and the seller. As with all communications, little is achieved if one does not understand the other. Let us therefore look first at the buyer.

The buying process, which governs the buyer, can be broken down into seven stages through which the buying mind goes on its way to reach a decision. These classic stages are often defined as:

1. I am important and I want to be respected.
2. Consider my needs.
3. How will your ideas help me?
4. What are the facts?
5. What are the snags?

6. What shall I do?
7. I approve.

Any sales attempt that responds unsatisfactorily to any of these stages is unlikely to end in an order. The buying mind has to be satisfied on each point before moving to the next and, to be successful, a sales presentation sequence must match the buying sequence and run parallel to it.

Table 6.1 shows the buying process alongside the sales objectives, what you are trying to achieve at each stage and the technique employed in any sales communication. The two keys to success are the process of matching the buyer's progression, and describing,

Table 6.1 The buying and selling processes

How people buy	Sales objective	How to sell: sales technique
I am important Consider my needs	To explore and identify customer's needs	Opening the sales interview
How will your ideas help me? What are the facts?	To select and present the benefits that satisfy the customer's needs	The sales presentation
What are the snags?	To prevent them, by anticipating snags likely to arise or handle objections so that the customer is satisfied with the answers	Handling sales objections
What shall I do? I approve	To obtain a buying decision from the customer or a commitment to the proposition presented	Closing the sale

selectively, the product and discussing it in a way that relates to precisely what the buyer needs. This may be a little different to the way 'product knowledge' is generally organized for you and this is therefore examined in the next section.

This kind of view of how selling takes place, or rather how buying and selling interact, was first set out by psychologists in the USA. However, it merely encapsulates common sense. This *is* how people weigh up whether to buy or not. The only thing that changes is the nature of what is being sold and the detail of the buying decision.

Some of the examples at the start of this chapter show what is virtually impulse buying. For instance, the waiter says, 'Another drink?' and the buyer's mind considers for only a split second before agreeing or not. At the other end of the scale, a buyer making a decision regarding a major purchase will weigh up many factors and attempt to do so objectively, though where competitors are evenly matched, technically or factually, the final element of the decision can often be subjective. Who *seems* best? Who is most trustworthy? And, of some importance, who does the buyer like best?

Incidentally, 'like' is best regarded as a bonus, that is it helps, but many will do business on the basis of mutual respect rather than liking you and you should not rely on those who think you are a wonderful person being sufficient to produce the quantity of business you want.

If expertise is involved, whether you sell a specialized service such as some sort of consultancy, or offer a service linked to products such as recommending and supplying computer equipment, software and systems, then there are particular points to bear in mind:

- selling yourself is part of the process (or more so than usual), so asking questions to identify client needs are key;
- clients cannot test services in advance and therefore want reassurance that you understand them and their problems, that you are reliable and that you are expert/professional;
- how they would describe their position and requirements.

Such factors are a part of every sales encounter, but are especially important in this area. In all cases the sequence shown in Table 6.1 can act as a guide to progress.

In all successful sales the buyer and the seller would have gone through this sequence stage by stage. If the attempt to sell, which just as often begins with an attempt to buy, is unsuccessful, it will be found that some part of the sequence of the customer's thinking and decision making has been missed or dealt with inadequately.

Early on, because the customer needs to go through other stages, you may not always be able to aim for a commitment to buy, but you must have a clear objective on which to 'close'. This may be to get the customer to allow you to send literature, to fix an appointment for a representative to call, or to provide sufficient information for a detailed quotation to be prepared. Whatever your objective is, however, it is important to know and be able to recognize the various stages that lie ahead. With any customer contact (by telephone or letter, as well as face-to-face), you must identify the following:

- What stage has been reached in the buying process?
- Does your selling approach match it?
- If not, why not?
- What do you need to do if the sequence does not match?
- Has a step been missed?
- Are you going too fast (or slowly)?
- Should you backtrack in the sequence?
- Can your objectives still be achieved or were they the wrong objectives?
- How can you help the buyer through the rest of the buying process?

Naturally, the whole buying process is not always covered in only one contact between a company and a customer. Every phone call or meeting does not result in a sale, but neither does it result in a lost sale. Some stages of the selling sequence have to be followed up in each sales contact, but the logic applies equally to a series of calls, which form the whole sales approach to each customer. For a customer who is unsure, or a sale of great complexity and expense, there may be numerous contacts to cover just one of the stages before the buyer is satisfied and both can move on to the next stage. Each call or contact has a selling sequence of its own in reaching the call objectives. Each call is a part of an overall selling sequence aimed at reaching overall sales objectives.

Planning the selling sequence is therefore as much a part of planning a sales meeting as it is of sales planning, but only rarely does a call take place exactly as planned. Knowing and using the sales sequence and being able to recognize stages of the buying process are, however, invaluable as you move through an unpredictable meeting and if you are to realize your potential and achieve positive sales results. Thus, everyone in the organization needs to be able to deal effectively with all calls and pass on those that will be completed by others, such as the sales person, in the organization.

With this basic appreciation of the buyer and what is directing their reactions, we can look closer at the key areas of the sales approach.

USING PRODUCT INFORMATION EFFECTIVELY

Identifying with the buyer, in order to recognize the stages of the buying process and to match them with a parallel selling sequence, must extend to the presentation of the sales proposition. Nowhere is this more important than in the way you look at the product or service you are selling.

Product knowledge is too often taken for granted by companies and salespeople. Sadly, experience of hearing hundreds of salespeople talking unintelligible gibberish does not support this complacency. Salespeople are often given inadequate product knowledge and what is given is slanted towards the company, not the customer. Managers are often still heard to say proudly, 'Everyone joining us spends six months in the factory, to learn the business', but many then emerge with no better idea of what the product *means to the customer*. Everyone with any role to play in sales-oriented customer contact must consider the product, and all that goes with it, from the customer's point of view. In a small company this means rapid, precise and appropriate briefing for all staff involved in the sales process.

Don't sell products, sell benefits

If you get into the habit of seeing things through the customer's eyes, you will realize that you do not sell special promotions, 'free' trial offers or fancy wrappings. You do not really sell products either. You sell what customers want to buy.

Customers don't buy promotions or products, they buy benefits

But what are benefits? Benefits are what products, promotions or services *do* for the customer. What the products are is not as important as what they *do for* or *mean* to the customer.

For example, a person does not buy an electric drill because they want an electric drill, but because they want to be able to make holes. They buy holes, not a drill. They buy the drill for what it will do (make holes). And this in turn may only be important to them because of a need for storage and a requirement to put up shelving.

When you realize this, your selling becomes more effective and also easier. You do not have to try to sell the same product to a lot of different people, but you meet each person's needs with personal benefits.

Benefits are what the things you sell can do for each individual customer – the things they want them to do for them. Different customers buy the same product for different reasons. Therefore, you must identify and use the particular benefits of interest to them.

What a product 'is' is represented by its 'features'. What a product 'does' is described by its 'benefits'

If this distinction is forgotten, then the things that are important to a customer will not always be seen as important from the seller's viewpoint, particularly if they have had little or no sales training. The result can, understandably, end up in a conflict of priorities. The customer is concerned, first, foremost and throughout with the customer. A close second comes the customer's needs and how they want them satisfied – and only then does the customer focus on a particular seller, their company and the prospect of buying from them. Whereas the seller starts, similarly, by thinking about themselves, their product or service and the company that produces it and only then about what it can do for customers generally and, last, for any individual customer.

This may be an inevitable reflex, but it must be moved away from if selling is to stand a real chance of being successful. The introspective approach is both the problem and the opportunity.

The customer is most unlikely to see things from the seller's point of view. Everyone is, to themselves, the most important person in the world. Therefore, to be successful, the seller has to be able to see things from the customer's point of view and demonstrate through words and actions that they have done so. The seller's chances of success are greater if they can understand the needs of the people they talk to and make them realize that they can help them to fulfil those needs (hence: 'Helping people to buy').

Achieving all this comes down to the correct use of benefits. In presenting any proposition to a customer, even simply recommending a product in reply to a query, you should always translate what you are offering into what it will do.

Often a company, and those who write the sales literature, grow product-oriented, and gradual product development can reinforce this attitude by adding more and more features. It is only a small step before everyone is busy trying to sell the product on its features alone. It is interesting to note that often, when this happens, advertising and selling become more and more forceful, with the features being given a frantic push, as passing time reveals that there has been no great rush to buy.

One example that is familiar to everyone is the audio market. Stereo equipment, in particular, is almost always promoted on features only. Masses of technical terms, most of them meaningless to the majority of end-users, dominate advertisements and brochures, while the visual communication is based entirely on the appearance of the amplifier, speakers or turntable. Yet what people want from a stereo set is good sound and reliability – years of listening pleasure. You can probably think of other examples: cameras, computers, photocopiers and even cars.

With competitive products so often being very similar in performance even selling benefits can be difficult, and choice may ultimately revolve round secondary elements, even peripheral factors. It is then not minor features that must be stressed, but their benefits. It is the balance of factors – large and small – upon which customers must finally base their choice.

In 'business-to-business' selling (to other companies rather than to individual customers), it is more important than ever to concentrate on benefits rather than on features, some of which are simply inherent to the product and others that may be little more than gimmicks. Features are only important if they support benefits that the customer is interested in.

Deciding to concentrate on benefits is only half the battle, however. They have to be the right benefits. In fact, benefits are only important to a customer if they describe the satisfaction of the customer's needs. Working out the needs and then the benefits means being 'in the customer's shoes'.

Who are the customers, what are their needs?

To know what benefits to put forward, you must know that the customer's needs are. And to know them, you have to know exactly who the customer is. Very often, the customer you deal with is the user – the person who will actually use the product. But, frequently, the direct customer is a purchaser or a decision-maker who is not the user. This is most common in business-to-business selling, when a buying department is often responsible for ordering. In consumer products, a manufacturer may sell to a wholesaler, the wholesaler to a retailer, and it is only the retailer who actually sells to the users.

Naturally, the requirements of the end-user will also be of interest to the various intermediaries, but the best results are going to be obtained if you can bear in mind the needs of both the buyer and the user and the differences between their various needs. To do this, it's convenient to use a product feature/benefit analysis, which also helps to differentiate features and benefits. Something of this process is shown in Table 6.2.

Thus, with a likely customer need firmly in mind, think about what you sell from the customer's point of view and list benefits and features, _starting with the benefits_. A list of isolated features is no problem. This thinking is simply a prompt, putting the right approach, sequence of explanation and words into your mind. Such an analysis can be produced for each product or for a product range, and is perhaps particularly useful for new products. Again, this is an exercise that can be shown within an office, or section, to spread the task and help everyone to learn just what is a feature and what is a benefit. It can act as a checklist and prompt the right approach.

Note that not all the needs will be objective ones. Most buyers, including business ones, also have subjective requirements bound up in their decisions. The pie chart in Figure 6.1 illustrates this concept: the line does not touch either axis as _no_ product is bought

Table 6.2 Benefits and features examples

Family car

Need	Low cost – not expensive to run
Benefit	Good miles per gallon figures
Feature	Efficient engine design/fuel injection/aerodynamic profile

Venue for a wedding reception

Need	Memorable
Benefit	Wedding photographs that people will love
Feature	An attractive 18th century country house hotel with beautiful gardens

A cooker

Need	Must cope with the family
Benefit	Will grill six steaks at one time
Feature	A 200 square inch grill pan

An accountant

Need	Cost-effective
Benefit	The right work with no disruption and at minimum cost
Feature	A computer-assisted audit

Note: This approach also reduces the likelihood of using too much confusing jargon. For instance, digital circuitry may make a roving telephone more efficient, but that description is both a feature and jargon. Saying it is crystal clear and will work equally well in every room in a large house, because of the digital circuitry, starts with benefits, uses the feature to add credibility and is truly descriptive.

---

on an entirely objective or subjective basis. Sometimes, even with technical products, the final decision can be heavily influenced by subjective factors, perhaps seemingly of minor significance, once all the objective needs have been met.

By matching benefits to individual customer needs you are more likely to make a sale, for a product's benefits must match a buyer's needs. The features are only what gives a product the right benefits.

By going through this process for particular products and for segments of the range, and matching the factors identified to

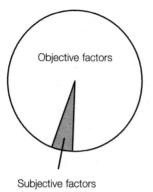 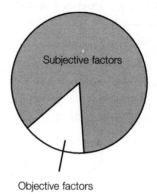

eg Industrial or technical purchases   eg 'Impulse buys' – fashion products, confectionery and cigarettes

(Note: In fact most products/services are a more equal mix of the two extremes.)

Figure 6.1 The nature of the reasons for buying

customer needs, a complete 'databank' of product information from the customers' viewpoint can be organized.

USING THE BENEFIT APPROACH

With competitive products becoming increasingly similar, more buyers quickly conclude that their main needs can be met by more than one product. Other needs then become more important. For instance, a buyer needing a fax machine is likely to find a number of them that will do the job required and which also cost virtually the same. The deciding factors will then become availability, service and repair facilities, and so on.

As a seller you can look at the 'features' of the organization itself and be ready to convert them to benefits for customers, in the same way as you can practise finding benefits for the full product range. Such features are all sources of benefits for customers. Four main sources of benefits and their aspects are shown in Table 6.3. Each item listed in the table could be a source of benefit to potential customers, which would help to make them an actual customer. In reality it is the detail that gives them power. For example, in terms of staff: it may be the ability of a computer consultant to explain in a way that makes matters clear and gives confidence that is valued by buyers, rather than some academic measure of knowledge. By 'thinking benefits' and by seeing things from the customer's point of view, everyone can make a real contribution to sales and company profitability.

Table 6.3 Four main sources of benefits

Products	design	storage
	price	workmanship
	delivery	credit
	appearance	stocks
	packaging	
Services	speed	training
	availability	advertising
	credit	merchandising
	after-sales service	pre-sales advice
Companies	time established	labour relations
	reputation	size
	location	policies
	philosophy	financial standing
Staff	knowledge	availability
	skill	training
	character	specialists

'Thinking benefits' is at the heart of sales technique. But it can be killed most easily by the use of jargon (professional slang), which can confuse anyone unfamiliar with it. Jargon comes in two forms:

1. *Technical or industrial jargon.* You should always let the customer be the first to use it. Technological complexities have already led to thousands of new words and phrases in business and industry,

and introducing still more new terms seldom helps. But worst of all is the possibility that the customer will not know what you are talking about or will form the wrong impression, yet hesitate to admit it.

2. *Company jargon.* It is even more important to avoid company jargon, for here the customer will be on very unfamiliar ground. There is a world of difference between 'We'll do a sales/stock return compo and the computer chappie will feed into the fourth floor, so we can let you know very shortly' and, 'To answer your query, we'll have to do a comparison of the sales and stock return movements. The quickest way will be to ask for a computer printout which head office will forward to us. I'll contact you with the answer in a week or 10 days' time.'

Company jargon can affect everything you deal with and even simple phrases can cause trouble. For example, delivery is one area for potential misunderstanding. Promising 'immediate delivery' might, in your terms, mean getting the product to the customer within a week, since normal delivery might take three weeks. But what if the customer is in an industry where 'immediate delivery' is jargon for 'within eight hours'? He is almost bound to get the wrong impression.

Jargon tends to be used as a reflex, out of habit, and its overuse, without consideration of its appropriateness, is worth guarding against.

Of course there is more to selling than simply talking benefits. You must be prepared, make a good first impression, be able to overcome or handle objections and see the whole process as leading up to 'the close', asking for the commitment to buy or proceed further. But nor is selling simply a matter of 'telling them': it has at least as much to do with identifying the individual customer's needs, upon which everything else that is done should be based. So it is about asking the right questions and listening to the answers.

ASKING THE RIGHT QUESTIONS

Early in the process it is important to find out what you want to know by asking the right questions in the right way. Two kinds of question make this easier:

■ *Open questions.* These are questions that cannot be answered by 'Yes' or 'No', but get the customer talking. These work best and produce the most useful information.
■ *Probing questions.* These go beyond enquiring about the background situation, to explore problems and implications and to identify real needs.

As an example, imagine a travel agent in conversation with a client:

Agent:	'What areas are currently your priority?'
Prospect:	'The Middle East is top priority for investigation but, short term, Germany has been more important.'
Agent:	'What makes that so?'
Prospect:	'Well, we're exhibiting at a trade fair in Germany. This will tie up a number of staff and eat up a lot of the budget. Our exploratory visit to the Middle Ease may have to wait.'
Agent:	'Won't that cause problems, seeing as you had intended to go earlier?'
Prospect:	'I suppose it will. With the lead times involved it may rule out the chances of tying up deals for this financial year.'
Agent:	'Had you thought of moving one of your people straight on from Germany to the Middle East?'
Prospect:	'Er, no.'
Agent:	'I think I could show some real savings over making two separate trips. If you did it this way, the lead time wouldn't slip. Would that be of interest?'
Prospect:	'Could be. If I give you some dates can we map something out to show exactly how it could be done?'
Agent:	'Certainly.'

This kind of questioning not only produces information but can also be used creatively to spot opportunities. It accurately pinpoints the prospect's real needs and allows an accurate response to them. Most prospects not only like talking about their own situation, but react favourably to this approach. They may well see the genuine identification of their problems and the offer of solutions to them as distinctly different to any other approach they have received from your competitors, which simply catalogues the product or service offered.

In this case, it also allows much better demonstration of two benefits that purchasers look for from travel agents: objectivity and expertise. The more these are apparent, the more the agency is differentiated from the competition.

Make no mistake, selling is a prime method of such differentiation. Attention to detail throughout the process can ensure you are seen as just that little bit different from – and better than – your competitors. The details of selling techniques are well worth exploring.

We now turn to another factor that goes closely with sales – service.

THE SERVICE ELEMENT

Selling must be backed by good service. Indeed, the two together can make an unbeatable combination. Good service is what customers want. Both a top hotel and McDonald's can rightly claim to offer good service, but operate in different contexts, where customers' views of what 'good service' means are very different.

Service comes not only from measurable factors such as delivering on time, but also from manner. For example, in my own company, the source of ring-binders used for the many courses and seminars we conduct was, for a while, influenced almost exclusively, in a commodity-type product area with many suppliers offering similar products, by the efficiency and customer orientation of one woman in the supplier's sales office. When she left them, our business was subsequently placed elsewhere. The antithesis of this is the 'abominable man' who too often seems to inhabit the sales office. He can destroy months of work by management and sales staff, miss opportunities and lose orders, or indeed customers, in a moment, maybe in one brief telephone call.

The role of back-up staff is investigated in Chapter 9, which reviews 'inside' sales activity. One area where service and sales can be made to overlap is with the process of encouraging repeat business.

CUSTOMER DEVELOPMENT

Long-term business comes less from customer loyalty, which is infinitely fickle, and more from working at it. The principles can be rapidly illustrated by returning to the example of the travel agent as used above.

Holding and developing customers

The travel agent knows that in winning more business travel the overall objective is not one order, but ongoing profitable business from clients in this area. Whether customers are retained, buy again and buy more is primarily dependent on two factors:

1. *Service.* It almost goes without saying, but promises of service must be fulfilled to the letter; if they are not, the customer will notice. A number of different people may be involved in servicing the account. They all have to appreciate the importance and get their bit right. If the customer was promised information by 3.30 pm, a visa by the end of the week, two suggested itineraries in writing and a reservation in a certain hotel at a particular price, then he or she should get just that. Even minor variations, such as information by 4 pm and a slight price difference on room rate, do matter. Promise what can be done. And do it 100 per cent.
2. *Follow-up.* Even if the service is first class, the customer must continue to be sold to after the order. In the case of our travelling businessman:

- Check with him after his trip.
- Check who else is involved in the next purchase. His secretary? Other managers?
- Ask more questions. When is his next trip? When should he be contacted again?
- Make suggestions. Can he book earlier? Would he like to take his wife on his next trip?
- Anticipate. Does he know fares are going up soon? Can he make the trip earlier and save money?
- Explore what else he might buy.
- Investigate who else in the company travels. Other staff, departments, subsidiaries?

■ See whether you can distribute holiday information among his staff.

■ Write to him, do not let him forget you. Make sure he thinks of you first.

A positive follow-up programme of this sort can maximize the chances of repeat business and ensure that opportunities to sell additional products or services are not missed.

So selling, effectively applied, is a vital tool in bringing in the business. If this means you doing it, make sure you build up personal sales skills: they can be learnt and developed with practice just like many other skills. If you have a sales team with some payment on results, this can be low cost in terms of the results it brings. Make sure it is well managed (sales people tend not to deliver 100 per cent performance without close management, but sales management is a whole separate topic, beyond the scope of this book).

What else makes selling effective? Well one factor, without any doubt, is persistence.

Sheer persistence

Once, I booked some training work with a large international company after 25 months of contact. Following the original meeting, I had one other meeting and perhaps a dozen other contacts (letter/ fax and telephone). This was neither time-consuming nor expensive. It was frustrating, however, and it would have been very easy not to make contact 'just once more' as the months went by. But it is always easier to sell to people you already know than start to again with a cold contact. So persistence pays. Of course, eventually you have to know when to give up and finally it may be made clear you should. In the meantime it's good policy to treat 'not yet' as exactly that. In my case, when confirmation came it was not in reply to any particular follow-up. It simply arrived; a two-line fax saying 'We will now go ahead' and asking for a particular course date.

In this example the delays were real and operational, but sometimes they are contrived obstacles. A friend once told me how he had phoned regularly over some months to try to get an appoint- ment with a particular prospect. Finally a meeting was agreed and – pleading lack of time – the prospect said 'I can only see you at 8 o'clock' (in the morning), though he knew it involved a journey of 200 miles to get to his office. My friend agreed. He got up very early and was there promptly at 8 am – and got the business. At the end of the meeting the customer apologized for the early start, and said 'I think, if you will put yourself out to that extent, I can trust your service.' It was a test, and a reasonable one from the point of view of the customer.

Persistence costs little and can give a positive image of commitment and service. Make no mistake, some of the available business goes, quite simply, to those who stay in touch.

There is one more factor which should be considered, and that is sheer nerve.

Sheer nerve

I once had to check out a resort hotel overseas for a series of courses I was mounting for a trade association. They wanted them run out of the city, so I set off on a Friday evening for the resort, with a booking, and all ready to check out a likely hotel for the event.

On the coach, I found myself sitting next to a man who turned out to be the manager of another nearby hotel. As we got into conversation he found out what I was doing. He gave a show of horror at the thought of where I was going and, to cut a long story short, persuaded me to stay with him – cutting off my protests about having a booking elsewhere by promising to telephone himself and cancel it (he did too). Not only did he get the immediate business but – he was also good at keeping in touch – more in the future.

There is a view of the successful salesperson being the type who sees a glass of wine as half-full, rather than half-empty. The above is illustrative of exactly what this means. By cultivating the habit of seeing opportunities everywhere and exploring them, even if a degree of cheek is necessary, you can, at no great cost, increase your contacts and your sales. The very worst that can happen is that some people will say 'No', which leaves you no worse off than if you had not approached them. And some will respond positively.

Both these last two techniques work and both are very definitely low cost. In fact selling is crucial to the low cost bringing in of business. Without a good sales 'strike rate', much of the time, effort and money spent on any sort of promotion will be wasted. A good strike rates means that, overall, fewer prospects and probably less promotion will be needed.

But selling is not the only personal skill that can bring in business without high cost; in the next chapter we examine another.

7

On Your Feet

Using formal presentations to win groups of customers

The human brain starts working the moment you are born and never stops until you stand up to speak in public.
SIR GEORGE JESSEL

Personal selling, the topic of the previous chapter, is a necessary and, in some ways, desirable method of obtaining business. It is often the final link in the promotional chain, the only technique that involves one-to-one contact. Many of its advantages, from simply putting a face to the organization to tailoring what is said to the individual prospect, can be applied to groups of people. Sometimes customers demand this – 'We would like you to present this to the board' – but clearly, if we can talk to 12 people, or 20 or even 200, then this may, provided it achieves its objectives, be a better use of scarce and valuable time. It can therefore be something worth organizing. If you have never done this you may not be able to envisage an application in which it would be useful, so we will start by reviewing some of the kinds of ways in which it is used. Some of these could have direct parallels in your business, while others may prompt additional ideas or variants that could work for you. We'll go on to look at how to make such events successful but, first, here are some examples.

Company A sells office equipment mainly to small businesses in and around the country town in which it is located. It has a showroom and works hard to get prospects to visit it. Prospects in smaller businesses, the managers, often the owners, find it difficult to get to it during working hours, even when equipment needs replacing. On Saturdays, however, most other offices in the block where Company A's showroom is located are empty and so is its car park, which is located close by the main shopping area. So it has hit on the idea of running regular demonstrations of equipment on Saturday mornings. In this business seeing is believing and demonstrations are important to the sale of many products. The offer in the letters it sends out is simple: 'When you visit the town for Saturday shopping, park free with us and attend our demonstration.' A presentation is set for a particular hour, though people can visit at any time and coffee is on the go throughout the morning. The attendance is good, since the offer of convenient free parking works well and direct orders do result, along with contacts that can be followed up later. This is a good idea, which cleverly uses a routine asset, the car park, to good effect.

Company B is a firm of accountants which, in common with many such firms, has successfully run a briefing at Budget time. This is in part social, in part informative. It gathers a group of clients together, if possible with some non-clients (a mix where those who know the firm will, by recommendation, help sell it to those who don't). One year the format was changed to a meeting, not on the day after the Budget but some 10 days later, commenting primarily on what had been announced. At this the partners were able to outline the implications for attendees, having had time to develop and document a *considered* view of any problems and opportunities that were significant for the future. In a service business something that presents the professional experience of the firm is very useful in generating leads. Any good idea may ultimately be improved by change, however successful it was at the start.

Company C is a publisher whose list includes textbooks designed either for use by schools or as additional reading for students. Details of these have to be communicated to teachers. In a big school, there may be a large number of teachers. Getting to them all may be difficult, certainly it will be time-consuming. So the company organizes a display area within the school (with permission of course); the time and format are announced and teachers are able to visit the display to inspect new titles and discuss their application with those manning the stand. Such events can commence with or include a formal presentation. This not only generates greater impact in a shorter time than trying to see everyone individually, but also helps identify those individuals who are worth a specific follow-up. Here is an example of an idea that can very well become accepted by customers as a regular event.

Company D produces a range of computer software and specializes in tailoring systems for use in business accounting. One of its senior people is, unusually, not only an expert in this area but also good at explaining it all to others who are less knowledgeable. The company has approached local banks that run regular briefings for business people, including those setting up a new business – a category Company D very much wants to sell to. Its expert is now the regular presenter on his topic at such events, which provide a number of opportunities throughout the year and allow him to meet people, many of whom are good prospects for the company. In this case, although initial arrangements must be made and the idea sold to the banks, the only cost is time.

Company E is an independent travel agency. It has a good high street site, but is in a competitive business. To increase awareness of both holiday ideas and itself as *the* place to book, it sets up a series of talks with local associations, the chamber of trade, the school parents' association and others. It is able to liaise with various national tourist bodies, which can supply films and other material, and with more local places too – one talk being on weekend breaks in the UK. In this way it can 'borrow' much of the expertise needed to put on the evening.

In all these cases the events create real sales possibilities, not only 'on the day', but also at subsequent meetings suggested or requested by the individuals attending. In some cases, for instance the input on behalf of the bank, the selling must be carefully positioned. It must occur through the information given out and not appear too 'pushy' or it will be seen as inappropriate. Nevertheless, the impact is immediate and direct. When people see you, or whoever represents the company, they form an immediate impression. They ask them-selves, is the person professional, expert, interesting, competent?

Whatever they look for in dealing with the kind of company you represent, they will judge whether such qualities are in evidence or not and do so quickly. First impressions last, as we all know all too well. Further, the impression gained is made up of all the elements the event makes visible to them and it is the total picture they take in. This includes the organization (even the invitation), where it is held, the arrangements and administration, the quality of display, visual aids and demonstration; in fact all the things that go on.

So, while this certainly qualifies as an effective and low cost approach, it must be well executed. Of course, the same applies to everything promotional, but there is an especial visibility about events, which means this is of particular importance, so much so that it is worth first spelling out the dangers.

WHAT MIGHT GO WRONG?

Dangers are everywhere. Some of the obvious ones include:

- slides that cannot be read from the back of the room;
- a speaker who cannot be heard (or, worse, who people wish they could not hear);
- poor quality handouts;
- a venue whose inefficiencies rub off on the organizer;
- poor time-keeping;
- an equipment demonstration which does not go to plan.

But others are less obvious. One meeting was always remembered by those attending. At the end of a slide show, when the projector was turned off, the evening had drawn in and all was in darkness in the hired room – no one knew where the light switch was. And any meeting can be spoiled by a poor presenter, or the opportunities it does produce being squandered by poor follow-up.

Despite such dangers, when all goes well the results can be considerable. Such events can be:

- cost-effective;
- manageable;
- directed precisely at specific groups of your potential customers;
- focused on individual aspects of the product/service.

They can have an immediate effect, or a longer-term one, or both. In addition, they can:

- reinforce relationships with existing customers;
- secure new customers;
- promote the full range of products/services;
- introduce new or varied products/services.

When they are well run they can draw attention to the company's efficiency, professionalism and good service. All that is necessary is that setting up and running such an event is approached systematically, implemented efficiently and followed up promptly.

The key is to conduct an event which you know will act to persuade attendees and which they will find appropriate (no inappropriate gimmicks) and useful. If, in addition, it strikes them as differentiating you from others by offering something better than your competitors, so much the better. None of this just happens; like so much in marketing it needs thought and planning.

THE PLANNING STAGE

Planning is important. Every detail must be right if the event is to give the impression and do the job you want. Two aspects must be considered: the event itself and all the arrangements, and the presentation to be made at it. We will look at these in turn.

Setting up the event

Why should an event be run at all? The idea has to come from somewhere and opportunities abound. It may be prompted by:

- topical external events, eg New Year, the coming summer holidays;
- internal developments, eg a new product or development deserving announcement;
- simply the need for promotion (with events linking to other techniques planned).

One of the first things to do, if not *the* first, is to appoint a 'stage manager'; in other words someone has to take overall charge of the way things will go or muddle will inevitably ensue. This person must:

■ set clear objectives (the more precisely you set out what you want to achieve, the more likely it is that the detail of the event can be put together in a way that will achieve the right results);
■ consider the mix of other promotional activity into which the event will fit and how such activities can support each other;
■ identify the people to be involved – internally in terms of who will do what (and also perhaps who should not, for various reasons, be involved) and externally – who will be asked to attend;
■ consider all physical aspects of the event, from where it will be held to what equipment may be necessary, etc;
■ make arrangements for all that will be needed for participants – refreshments, handouts, literature, etc.

And – very important – the 'stage manager' must keep an eye on the timing, scheduling all that needs to be done back from the date on which the event will be held to ensure everything is done in good time.

These responsibilities are worth examining individually.

Objectives

Without clear objectives the rationale for the event is in question. Objectives should reflect customer satisfaction. Your objectives alone, 'to sell the product range', are insufficient and too introspective. Objectives set with the customer in mind create a better chance of success for the event. For example good reasons might be stated as follows:

■ To present a demonstration of our equipment that will show how easy it is to operate and prompt attendees to ask for a trial use at their own premises (office equipment); or
■ To show the video and lay out guidelines that persuade managers attending they can make convenient and effective use of it in a training session, without lengthy preparation of their own input (training materials).

In addition, the objectives set should be compatible with whatever other promotional activity is scheduled for the same period, as apparent clashes of intention here will be noticed and may be taken as a sign of inefficiency, reflecting poorly on the business. Ultimately attendees will judge the success of any event by what it did for *them* and what is more they look at invitations in the same way, asking 'Will this be useful?' Your prospective customers are doubtless busy people and will not turn out for something unless they feel it will be genuinely useful. They will give it priority that fits it into their schedule if, even in the announcement, you can persuade them that they will:

- hear/see something useful;
- receive valuable handouts;
- like the venue;
- only have to give up a reasonable amount of time (at a convenient time);
- meet others who may be useful or interesting.

The promotional mix

Other chapters in this book examine the range of promotional techniques that you can use. Here we are concerned to be sure that there is no clash of activities with the techniques necessary to make the event a success and how these (there may be several) can best work together. Here are some examples:

- How will the event be announced? If, say, this will be done through a direct mail invitation, then what else might support this? For example, can a press release or newsletter act as advance warning? What about posters in your office/showroom, at the venue or elsewhere?
- How can any aspect of the event be used in other additional ways? For example, can a presentation or handout be cleverly adapted to create an article for a magazine or newspaper?

Such consideration should include the time before, during and after the event and the complexity can be sufficient to make the use of a simple planning chart useful. An example of a planning chart is shown in Figure 7.1. The information on such a form can be added to progressively as decisions are made and allows the interrelationship of different items to be seen clearly. If different colours are used, you can add details showing, for instance, not just when a press release needs to be sent, but when the copy needs finalizing and when it must be printed.

The people

Consider first you and your own people. The scale of involvement will clearly follow the nature and scale of the event. Sometimes one speaker is all there is, while on other occasions you need several, with someone to act as chairperson, plus a video, say. Selecting who will be involved must allow for the expertise people have, their presentation skills (all too often poor presentation skills mar an otherwise good event), and must relate also to their seniority (which may or may not be relevant) and certainly to their discipline in contributing – there is absolutely no room for someone who ignores vital deadlines.

As well as those who have an obvious role on the day, others may need to be involved in supporting roles. Tasks such as briefing and checking details with a chosen venue, preparing handouts/ literature, acknowledging requests to attend and acting as receptionist on the day all need to be done efficiently and impressively. Everyone involved will need briefing and this must be done in good time if all is to go well.

Secondly, you must give specific attention to potential invitees. These may be selected from one or more of the following groups:

- *Existing customers*, where ongoing contact is necessary to hold and develop their business with you; an event can provide an important part of that continuity. In addition, customers who know and think well of you will probably play a valuable role on the day as they mix with others and recount their good opinion of you.
- *Prospects*, or those who you intend to become customers. These may be people you are contacting for the first time or others you have had various attempts to persuade and for whom an event may be the final prompt to their becoming a customer (this may also include dormant customers from the past).
- *'Recommenders'*, that is intermediaries who are in a position to recommend you to others, in the way a local bank manager might recommend various other local services to someone opening a new business account. This is a category to identify carefully and with whom to keep regularly in touch.

PROMOTIONAL ACTIVITY PLANNING CHART		
Date	Overall planned activity	Event activity
January		
15	Newsletter	
February 1		Invitations sent press release
14	Advertisement	Telephone reminders to key prospects
16		
27		*DATE OF EVENT

Figure 7.1 Promotional activity planning chart

The venue

If you have the space on your premises and it is suitable, then you may have no need to look elsewhere. However, you may need to find somewhere to accommodate the event. Make a list of questions to ask to find out if a venue is really suitable:

■ Is it convenient (to participants and you, but participants are more important)? For example, is it near a station, does it have a car park?

■ Is it suitable for our event? Does it have the right facilities, equipment, etc and a business-like atmosphere?

■ Will participants like it and consider it suitable? Consider ambience and cost (too expensive and they may feel it reflects your prices).

All these questions focus rightly on the attendees, though there are other considerations for you and cost no doubt ranks high among them.

A good choice of venue can make or break an event. Time spent checking out a number of different venues to find what is most suitable and then in briefing the chosen one is time well spent. At this point a checklist approach may be useful and safest and will ensure that nothing is overlooked. An example is given in Figure 7.2.

If you are concerned with large events or want to be really thorough, a good reference here is the checklist published by the Meetings Industry Association (MIA), *Meeting with Confidence* (for further information telephone the MIA on 0386 858572).

Certainly you should always inspect the venue. Do so thoroughly, not just looking at the room and perhaps trying the food, but testing the acoustics and trying out any slides you plan to use to see that they will be clearly visible. Make sure you have the names of key people at the venue, particularly those who will be on duty at the time, and investigate important details, from how messages will be dealt with to whether they will supply you with copies of maps to guide participants safely there.

All the time this process must relate to your considered view of what is necessary for the event itself. Thus, specific details can be related to the venue as you check. For instance, do you need:

EVENT RESOURCES LIST			
Resources needed	Who is responsible	Deadline date	Comments
Venue 1 2 3 4 5 6			
Equipment 1 2 3 4 5 6			
Participants' kit 1 2 3 4 5 6			
On the day 1 2 3 4 5 6			

Figure 7.2 Event resources list

■ Display space?
■ Equipment, including microphone, slide projector, etc?
■ Signs (both directional and to highlight your name)?
■ To be able to control lights, heating or air conditioning from within the room?
■ An event office or separate reception area?

Have you considered everything to do with catering, allowing time appropriate to the food and discussion? Do you want buffet or sit down meals, or will light refreshments or just a drink be adequate? And watch everything linked to costs. How is the bar charged? What about telephones? Do you need to pay a deposit? What are the contractual implications (for instance if you have to cancel or numbers attending are other than expected)?

At this stage you ought to be clear about:

■ the date and time;
■ timing (a day, a few hours, breakfast or what?);
■ location;
■ the budget;
■ the equipment required;
■ access (can you set up in advance?).

You may want to summarize all this on a checklist form, such as the one shown in Figure 7.3.

Participants' kit

Not least among all the things to be arranged are the items that each invitee will need, as all this will have to be organized too. What people receive and take away must reflect the overall image you intend, and this starts with the invitation.

The invitation, whether letter, card or brochure (or a combination), must set the scene. As has already been said, the event must be persuasively described, remembering that people do not *have* to attend. A full picture of what's in it for them will help gain decisions to attend: they will want to know why they should attend and what attendance will give them. So the quality of this is vital.

Once people have arrived they may need a variety of documentation. You may want to provide a suitable folder or binder to accommodate this, designed for people to retain. In addition to

EVENT TIMETABLE

Time:	What will be done	How it will be done	Who	Resources and equipment	Comments
10.00 to 10.45	Introduction and lead into product demonstration	10 minutes introduction 15 minutes product description 10 minutes questions	P.F.	OHP slides Brochure distributed to participants	Finish on time or coffee will be cold.

Figure 7.3 Event timetable

handouts, product information fact sheets and technical specifications, you should consider other items such as:

- a clear timetable;
- a list of attendees (people like to know who is there and where they are from);
- questionnaires (to gather their opinions about the event);
- and, most important, clear and specific information about what to do next, how to order, obtain more information or arrange a personal meeting, for instance.

The quality of what is issued is important: a good quality binder (with your name and contact details on it) is more likely to be kept than a simple cardboard folder. The whole ensemble will make an impact, for good or ill, and this comes, in part, through attention to detail.

Planning is crucial. A successful event will never ensue from anything but careful planning and the dangers of failing to impress have already been mentioned. A planning schedule is worth putting on paper, along the lines of the form shown in Figure 7.4.

Together, the event timetable and planning schedule encapsulate the essentials and the detail flows from them. The organizer must approach the whole process with the attitude that nothing can be left out. If someone asks on the day for an aspirin, a pencil, change for the telephone or train times, then if it has not been thought of in advance, it may not be able to be provided and the impact of the overall event suffers just a little.

Further, every aspect of the event needs to be approached creatively. The example of the use of the free car park on a Saturday, mentioned earlier in this chapter, is a good one. Such ideas are worth searching for in every aspect of the event: if people go away feeling that they have experienced something unusual or particularly useful, if they feel it is different from other events they have attended, perhaps only in some detail, then they are more likely to respond positively, and that is the object of the exercise.

WHAT WILL BE PRESENTED?

The message and how exactly it is put over is central to any event and its presentation will represent the major portion of the time

EVENT PLANNING SCHEDULE				
Date due	Action	Who	Comments	Date Complete
1 March	Draft text for invitation letter	S.G.	To fit 2 sides A4 and match brochure	28 Feb

Figure 7.4 Event planning schedule

available. Before commenting further on how to make sure the presentations made are a real asset to your company, a brief consideration of the overall time involved is necessary.

The length of any event is likely to be a compromise. You need to consider the various parts of the event that make up the whole. How long is necessary for the following:

■ Reception of the attendees?
■ Introductions?
■ The session(s)?
■ Questions and discussion, both formal and informal (where these are placed is important, too, so beware of a session that dies for lack of planned participation)?
■ Breaks and refreshments?

With all these components you need to consider how long is necessary, how long will be thought necessary by those attending (these may not be the same) and how much time in total people are likely to give up willingly. They want their time valued, not an event that is strung out and becomes boring and time wasting, nor on the other hand something where brevity makes it insubstantial. Get the balance right and it will be appreciated and the event will go better.

With the overall duration in mind you can turn to the content, decide who will say and do what and how the sessions will fit together to provide variety and pace, as well as allowing the message to be got across. Then you can turn to the job of preparing the individual presentations themselves.

Make no mistake: people, organizations, proposals and much more are judged on the quality of presentations. People do not say, 'What an excellent scheme, what a pity it was poorly put over'; they say, 'What a rotten presentation, it must be a rotten scheme'. This may not be fair, but it's what happens. The only response is to recognize and accept it as real life and resolve to make excellent presentations.

And excellent presentations start with sufficient preparation and rehearsal. There can be no half-measures here, for there is too much at stake. Yet presentation is not everybody's 'bag'. If you do not see yourself as a star presenter, that may only be, in part, because you don't know enough about how to go about it. There are tricks of the trade, just as with so many skills, and how to do it well can be learnt. You may never be a great orator but, with a little study

and practice, you can surely do justice to a good business presentation.

So, if you plan to use this sort of promotion, take time to
become a good presenter. A broad outline is all there is space for
here, but you can read up on it (there are many useful books on the
subject, for example my own _30 Minutes Before a Presentation_ in
Kogan Page's excellent series of mini-books covers the essentials).
Or you can go on a course or even have personal tuition to help you
plan and rehearse real presentations before they are conducted live.
I do this on occasion not just for senior people in large companies,
but for individual business people who recognize the importance of
presentations to their business. Presentations are referred to in the
Video Arts film, _I wasn't prepared for that_, as 'the business equivalent
of an open goal'; an excellent description.

In considering the matter here it is, of course, not sufficient
for a presentation to be clear, understandable and lively – it must
also be persuasive (thus many of the techniques reviewed in Chapter
6 are relevant). The essence of a good presentation is that it should
be:

- _appropriate to the audience:_ bear in mind the group's seniority,
  knowledge of the topic and of you, and the perspective they bring
  to bear on the whole thing;
- _understandable:_ this is easy to underrate, for even if you know
  your topic well you have to think about how to get the message
  over – a clear sequence and structure, descriptive language and
  well-chosen visual aids, together with an avoidance of unneces-
  sary jargon will all help ensure the message gets over accurately
  and easily;
- _interesting:_ how something is said obviously has a bearing, but
  the most important aspect here is to ensure a focus on those
  attending and what their needs are – ultimately they will do
  business with you because they believe that what you offer is
  right for them. If you show them the benefits you can offer, then
  you are well on your way to a positive decision;
- _credible:_ they know _you_ think what you have to offer is good,
  but give them reason to believe there is more to it than that –
  using references, testimonials, tests and independent opinion to
  bolster your case;
- _two-way:_ this may seem like a contradiction in terms but you
  need feedback from the way the group looks and responds and

from the question sessions and informal conversations that form part of the total event.

TELL 'EM, TELL 'EM AND TELL 'EM

Beyond what has been said so far, a presentation needs a good structure. Basing it on the oldest of communications maxims that you should tell people what you are going to tell them (introduction), tell them (the main content) and then tell them what you have told them (summary) may sound simplistic but is excellent advice. Though each of the three sections will need organizing, listing key and subsidiary points, the whole thing starts to come together and all that is necessary is to set down what you plan to say in a form from which you can conveniently, once you are used to the message, speak. Incidentally, it is very much easier to speak fluently from notes than to try to read a prepared text. This never comes over well (an audience recognizes when something is being read and likes it less on principle) and besides it is curiously difficult to do. Experiment with a form of notes that suits you and you will find that the security they offer (and being well prepared) is a prime antidote to nerves.

The checklist below summarizes some of the key aspects of making an effective presentation. Don't embark on anything promotional of this sort without a degree of preparation, practice and rehearsal; the time it takes is always worth while and you know what, in your own case, is at stake.

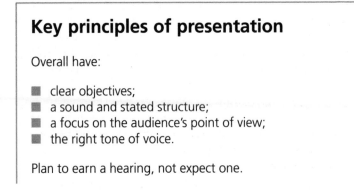

Key principles of presentation

Overall have:

- clear objectives;
- a sound and stated structure;
- a focus on the audience's point of view;
- the right tone of voice.

Plan to earn a hearing, not expect one.

The beginning

This must respect the audience and make it clear that you will be accurately directing your message at them and their needs. Here you must:

- get off to a good start;
- gain people's attention;
- begin to build rapport;
- make the group want to listen by starting to satisfy expectations, yet ensure they keep an open mind for what is to come;
- position yourself as the speaker appropriately (eg, as confident, expert, credible);
- state your theme, outline how you will go through it (structure) and make it clear this will suit them (you may also feel it is appropriate to say how long you will take if the timetable does not – and then stick to that time).

The middle

This is the longest section and it must:

- maintain and develop interest;
- develop the case through a logical sequence of sub-themes and points;
- illustrate as necessary, with descriptive language and visual aids;
- overcome doubts and scepticism, anticipate specific objections and deal with them and ensure that the message you are building is seen as being of value to those listening.

The end

You need to finish on a high note, maybe with a flourish. The concluding part of the presentation must:

- summarize and pull together the arguments;
- stress the benefits to the group;
- make clear what action is now appropriate (and often actually ask for a commitment);
- finish on a memorable note.

Throughout the presentation, how you appear and the animation with which you go about the task are just as important as how you sound. The *language* and *gestures* you use must be clear, natural, positive and courteous, and place emphasis on the key points so that the overall impression is of out-and-out *professionalism*. Your goal is to get your professional approach prompting people to think: 'This is the sort of person I could do business with.'

REHEARSAL

Don't think this is going too far, especially if two or more people have to work – seamlessly – together. Rehearsal simulates the real occasion, allows you to try out individual elements (whether a description, a quip or a gesture) and builds confidence and competence like nothing else.

So, present to a group of colleagues, even recording what you do (on video or audio), practise using visual aids (something like an overhead projector takes a moment to get used to) and think ahead, anticipating, planning and rehearsing the answers to questions as well as the formal presentation. Rehearsal should not stilt flexibility; rather, it helps make it easier to digress and return to something you are sure of to create a dynamic whole.

ATTENTION TO DETAIL

The presentations may be the core of the event, but other factors also contribute to its success. Some of the other details you need to consider include the following.

The invitations

The numbers attending are vital. Too many may be as bad as too few, but getting the kind of numbers you want is something not to be taken lightly. Whatever the format of the invitations, cards, brochures or letters (all usually used with an easy reply device), they will ideally:

- be sent out far enough ahead of the event date;
- look professional and well designed;
- reflect your house style;
- be clear, accurate and, above all, persuasive (getting the message right is more likely to be neglected than the design – both are important), so it must tell people what they will get from it, not simply what will happen at it;
- be personal: use their name and yours;
- ask for all the information you want (don't forget to ask for their job title, for instance, so that you know exactly who is present); and
- as has already been said, make replying really easy, perhaps with an option to phone or fill in a card (reply paid).

Acknowledgements

You will almost certainly need to confirm attendance to those who reply. Do this efficiently and don't forget details such as maps, car park tickets, etc.

The venue

This has already been mentioned as being important. Every detail is vital and briefing meetings and checks may be necessary to get everything buttoned down tight. Always check, for example, that:

- arriving attendees can find their way (signing in);
- all equipment is tested and working (one upside-down slide is one too many, count the chairs, try the spare bulb, sound test the microphone and then do it all again);
- name cards are ready (people like to be able to see who else is there) in A–Z order, and that there are some spares;
- your own staff are in place, well turned out and absolutely sure what is expected of them.

A pleasant welcome

First impressions matter. Address people by name as they arrive, have tea or coffee, or whatever the time of day makes appropriate, ready. Also make clear what they need to do: where to go first, where to sit, whether to wear a badge, etc.

Timing

Keeping to the schedule looks efficient and you want to look efficient. So start on time (even if only to make a short announcement to say you propose to give latecomers five more minutes). Follow the timetable during the meeting and make it known that you are doing so. Similarly, *never* overrun. This is resented and you run the risk of an event finishing in disarray as some people begin to slip away. Speed and promptness are part of timing. For example, if there is something to give out, do so quickly (this has implications for staffing numbers).

Finally, always thank people for attending and for their time (though don't make this the last thing you do; remember the need to finish strongly). If you move on to informal sessions – over drinks, say – have some clear lead-ins ready to prompt individual conversations with those attendees you meet personally. 'Nice to see you' – 'You too' – doesn't take you far. Use issue-led questions to get on to the right ground: 'Tell me, how do you cope with this question of X we were discussing?' is far more likely to lead to a useful conversation, one that gets them talking.

The chairperson

If you need a chairperson, perhaps to link two or three presenters or control a session of questions and discussion, then this role has to be well handled. It will again make the overall impression more powerful. Like a number of the arrangements and other factors mentioned, this is something that may be largely unnoticed when it goes well, but which can stand out as a glaring problem if it is not well handled.

BEWARE OVERKILL

Persuasiveness can, if overdone, be seen as being pushy and thus self-defeating. So there is an important caveat here, that striving too hard can end up producing nothing. For many, especially those without any background on the sales side, there is a fear of becoming too pushy, which must be overridden. In reality, these people can afford to be a good bit more positive before there is any chance of prospective customers switching off because they find their approach too pushy.

On the other hand, there is a danger that, given a whole event to use to impress a group, the event itself becomes of little value and people feel the only message is that they should spend money to find out more. If the event itself is genuinely useful in its own right, then the chances of sales following seem actually to increase. Consider a couple of examples. A small accountancy firm and a computer firm join with a local bank to put on an event that will assist small businesses setting up for the first time. If the message their nominated speakers put over is, in the case of the accountant, that the accounting and tax problems are dire and that only retaining their firm will make it easy, then people are suspicious and do not tend to look to the speaker for help. If the computer expert can actually offer good advice, something people can use without further reference to the speaker, not only is their expertise demonstrated, but the credibility of their advice is on show as well and people are more likely to get back to them to sort out their other problems – on a paid basis.

The balance here is important and worth actively considering when you are arranging the format and the presentations for a particular event. It is the excellence of what is done that makes the impression. Another example is product demonstration. Imagine someone is selling, say, a fax machine. What do those watching the demonstration look for? If the sales person goes to the prospective purchaser's office, the machine should be set up and ready to demonstrate fast (the prospect is a busy person). At an event, you can have everything ready in advance, so what is done must:

- be clear and understandable;
- move logically through the detail;
- perform 100 per cent right – first time;
- make those watching feel they could do it;
- project an appropriate image (quality, value for money, whatever is right);
- cope with the location (not constantly saying, 'Of course, it's easier in an office');

- focus on customer needs, not simply listing features;
- back up performance data with proof;
- be presented in an interesting way;
- be impressive to all involved (eg a fax might be shown to bosses and secretaries);
- tell and show benefits throughout.

Again this makes the point that the way it is done is a good advertisement for the person doing it. Attendees may not want the fax but, seeing a good demonstration, may think of the demonstrator next time they do need to consider some kind of office equipment. This is exactly the kind of effect one is after from events, one that can be as valuable longer term as in the immediate aftermath of the event.

After all this and having organized an event and put over a first-class presentation – something you are truly satisfied with on the day – you cannot just leave it there. What happens after the event is one of the most important contributions to the value that will ultimately be gained from it.

ACTION AFTER THE EVENT

There are things to be done after the event. A good deal of time and effort goes into such a function, even a small one, and the instinctive reaction when it's all over may be to heave a big sigh of relief and pour a large gin and tonic. However, it's not quite over yet: two things need attention. First, you need to assess – objectively – how it all went.

What can be learnt from it?

If events are to be any part of your promotional armoury, then learning from experience is important. This is somehow more obvious if things have gone wrong, but just as valuable when they have not. You will want to use again what worked well, or maybe make something good just a little better next time.

Perhaps the key thing to do is make an honest appraisal of the presentations, whoever did them. It does not matter whether it was you, a guest or the most senior person in your company; questions need to be asked constructively to see that an even better impression is given next time. Your review should follow the kind of points listed below:

- Was sufficient preparation and rehearsal carried out?
- Did the presentation make immediate impact?
- Was there an effective summary?
- Could the slides be seen clearly at the back of the room?

Other areas worth reviewing include the venue and other arrangements, for example:

- What went well?
- What went less well or caused a problem?
- How about time-keeping?
- What about equipment?

All this should be undertaken with an eye on making the next event better still. Because the time after an event is always busy, there is a real temptation to put such matters on one side. Much more tends to be got from such a review when matters are fresh in the mind and it is well worth taking a few minutes to consider all this, perhaps with the aid of the questionnaires you asked your audience to fill in.

Further promotional/sales action

An event cannot be viewed in isolation. It is probably part of an ongoing communication with the people involved. The question is, therefore, what contact is appropriate next? This should be considered on an individual basis; numbers attending events are rarely so large that you cannot do this, so consider:

- those invited but not attending;
- those attending;
- those attending and spoken to personally;
- those expressing specific or general interest.

Consider, too, the nature of the people in these categories. Do you know them? Are they potential customers or recommenders? What is their potential in terms of the size of business that could be forthcoming from them? All may need different action. It is better to send six or seven different kinds of letter, phone some people and approach some in other ways that will be seen as appropriate by those you are contacting, than to opt for a standard follow-up and find your ultimate response is less. The small additional time that may be necessary is always worth while.

Key within this is the specific response to specific requests. Any individual interest and particularly individual action promised must be actioned promptly and efficiently. It must be entirely clear within your company who is doing what, or things can fall between the cracks as everyone starts to catch up on their backlog of work.

To ensure not only the follow-up but the following through of leads (they may, after all, take a number of actions to convert into business), a form for individual enquiries may be useful. An example is shown in Figure 7.5. As you can see, the form can be very simple, but it allows not only a record to be kept, but also a prompt to be made, as the last entry should always be what is *planned to do next* to progress the interest. The very existence of such a document focuses attention on the action necessary.

Finally, it's easy to find yourself looking back months later and making very general comments, 'That was a good event', 'Lots of people attended', which are not so very useful when you're trying to decide whether to repeat it. So, a summary of results, including longer-term ones (how much business can be traced back to the event?) is worth while. A form may help this too; see Figure 7.6. If this is filed with copies of other documents, such as the invitation that went out, then a later review can appraise what happened on a factual basis.

A WORTHWHILE METHOD?

Events such as those described in this chapter do not suit every business, but – in one form or another – they do suit many. Although they take some setting up and the first one undertaken may be somewhat daunting, they need not be expensive compared to what they can achieve and can be a very effective method of promotion and selling. Remember that if costs are paramount, finding a partner may make sense, at least initially.

EVENT ENQUIRY SCHEDULE	
Event:	Date held:

Request for action/information

_____

_____

_____

From:

Name _____

Job title _____

Organization _____

Address _____

_____

Tel _____ Fax _____

Date	Record of Action

Figure 7.5 Event enquiry form

EVENT RESULTS RECORD

Event:	Date held:

Venue: _____ Comments: _____

_____

_____

Speakers: _____

Equipment used: _____

_____

Lists used to invite attendance: _____

_____

_____

Number attending: _____

COSTS		LEADS	Outcome
	£	Total number: _____	
Budget	_____	1 _____	
Actual costs	_____	2 _____	
_____	_____	3 _____	
_____	_____	4 _____	
_____	_____	5 _____	
_____	_____	6 _____	
_____	_____	7 _____	
_____	_____	8 _____	
_____	_____	9 _____	
Total	_____	10 _____	
Variance +/– £	_____	11 _____	
Comments:	_____	12 _____	
_____		13 _____	
_____		14 _____	

Figure 7.6 Event results record

With some thought you may be able to put on something that works well for your business. The response is then directly measurable. You can see how many people turn out. You can judge at the end how people felt it went. The feedback may be positive. The follow-up action can make it more so, and ensure still more comes from what has been done. It's always particularly satisfying when business results from something where you really feel you actively made it all happen.

8

Selling at a Distance

Using the telephone to find, secure and develop customers

*Well, if I called the wrong number, why
did you answer the phone?*
JAMES THURBER

The telephone is a powerful weapon in the sales armoury. As Chapters 6 and 7 dealt with the psychological processes of buying and selling and as the techniques of selling face-to-face are essentially similar however the contact is made, this chapter focuses on where and how the telephone has a role to play in that process.

The telephone is ubiquitous. We grow up with it and most of us take it for granted; so much so that one psychologist recently coined the acronym CCS – compulsive communication syndrome – for those (naming no names) who cannot stop phoning. Yet its use in selling can, all too easily, be taken for granted, and without care it can be less effective or even have a negative effect in terms of image. Alternatively, it can be found awkward, or embarrassing, with the same result and, in both cases, possible sales go by default.

This is not, on reflection, surprising. As a means of communication the telephone can be underestimated in terms of its difficulty.

Its key characteristics, at least until videophones are widely available, is that it uses voice only. This may be an obvious point, but one which makes a great difference to both understanding (or lack of it) and to perception. This factor alone negates some uses of the phone, for passing on complex information or technicalities, for instance. As an everyday example, try to explain to someone how to tie a shoelace without using gestures. It's difficult, if not impossible. More pertinently, think of companies you deal with, suppliers perhaps, but which you have not visited – what impression do you have of their office built up from your telephone contacts with them? Do you, in your mind's eye, see an efficient, streamlined, modern office; a smartly turned out person at the other end with all the facts at their fingertips and the systems to back them up? Or do you see an untidy, chaotic mess? Whichever it is, the vision is likely to be a clear one. You feel you really know what they are like; and others will have the same thoughts about your organization.

We return to the service aspects of this in Chapter 9 where we look at the sales office. Here, we are concerned specifically with the use of the telephone in a real sales role. It can, of course, be used to do many different things, from simply checking the name of a sales contact, to securing the final agreement in a major deal. There are three main uses on which we will focus here: prospecting and making appointments (important when a sale can only be made face-to-face); 'keeping in touch', adding purpose and persistence to such reminders; and actually taking orders.

PROSPECTING

Prospects may arise in many ways. They may be those who respond to your advertisements or they may be more actively sought out (some ideas on this appear in Chapter 6). Here let's assume you have received an enquiry – a tentative one, of which you know little, perhaps a reply card or a coupon returned for more information.

You want to meet with the enquirer and you decide to telephone to try to set up an appointment. How do you proceed?

■ *First, always do some research.* Check their letterhead, look them up in a directory, read the trade press if you deal with one industry. If it's clear to them as you start to speak that you know nothing about them, everything else will be that much more difficult.

- *Next, have clear objectives in mind.* This may seem obvious, namely to sell them something. But what is the first contact for? To obtain information or to make an appointment? If the latter, when and where will that be? At their office or factory? At an exhibition or demonstration? You need to have the specifics clearly in mind before you lift up the receiver.

- *When do you want to see them?* Not just 'as soon as possible', but at a time and date that suits your schedule and productivity. Beware of suspect 'received wisdom' such as, 'No buyer wants to see you before 10 am' when in fact some will not only happily see you at 8.30 am, but you are likely to have an uninterrupted hour until their switchboard opens. Neither should you believe that, 'No buyer will see you after 4 pm or on Fridays, or when there is an R in the month.' In fact everyone's habits are different and you simply risk restricting your opportunities if you make unwarranted assumptions.

With the answers to the foregoing in mind it is now time to think about actually making an appointment. Ultimately, even if a letter has been sent, you will soon find yourself on the telephone. The phone is a form of communication that presents both problems and opportunities. It's not everyone's favourite kind of call, but you will get a better success rate; and if you do that, at every stage, you will sell more in the end. Before we speak to the prospect, however, there is still something else to consider.

Getting through to the right person

This is not just a matter of defeating the mechanical gremlins of the telephone company and the more modern hazards of voicemail and automated systems, but being able to make direct contact with the decision-maker. This difficulty alone can get sales people off to an uneasy start in prospecting. Switchboards and secretaries are often past masters at spotting, and refusing, anyone who is selling. Some simple rules will help you overcome this problem.

In 'cold calling' prior research may have given you the name you want. If not, always ask for the name first and then ask to be put through, for instance:

| *Salesman:* | 'May I have the name of your chief accountant?' |
| *Operator:* | 'You mean Mr Morris?' |

Then ask to speak to him. You may be put straight through and you will know as he answers 'Morris here' that you have the right person, avoiding the need to check who he is as he answers. Operators and secretaries will often put a call through to a department or assistant first rather than the manager himself.

Alternatively, more questioning may follow:

| *Operator:* | 'Who is calling Mr Morris?' |
| *Salesman:* | 'Mr Roberts.' |

At this stage you may be put through, particularly if you say your name confidently. The same applies to the question, 'What company are you with?' You should answer confidently and without volunteering any extra information.

The really protective switchboard operator will then ask, 'What are you calling about?' Avoid clichés and dishonest answers, like 'I'm conducting a research survey.' Instead, describe briefly and comprehensively what you want to discuss (*not* what you want to sell), eg: 'I need to talk to Mr Morris about computer stationery for the new EDP installations at your branches.' A secretary/operator is unlikely to want to get involved in the detail of what may by then sound a little complicated and you should, at this point, get through.

For regular or follow-up contacts the same principles apply, at least if there remains a chance your prospect would rather not speak to you. It is useful to refer back to past events, eg 'I agreed with Mr Morris when I saw him last month that I would call this week.' Only phrase it this way if it *was* agreed; alternatively say, 'I said to Mr Morris...' or, having written suggesting you call him on a particular day, 'Mr Morris is expecting to hear from me today.' (This kind of approach can also be used as a follow-up to the right kind of phrase in a selling/prospecting letter.)

If the buyer is not at the office, the secretary may offer to help or take a message. The most useful piece of information you can obtain is when the contact will be available to take a call. Ask, 'May I call back this afternoon?' or, 'Will he be available tomorrow morning?' This saves you time in further wasted calls and means that you can tell the operator next time, 'I arranged with Mr Morris's secretary to call him at about this time.'

Whatever kind of call you are making, it's necessary to get through to the right person; what follows depends on the nature of the call and your objectives.

Making the appointment

Whoever you are calling, whether it's someone who has seen a brochure, responded to an advertisement or mail shot, or simply a 'cold prospect', think about the call before you make it.

Before you even dial the prospect's number, you must have at hand (or on screen) the following:

■ all customer information available to date, including any 'personal hints', which can help avoid simple gaffes such as the wrong pronunciation of someone's name;
■ information on your availability for appointments;
■ a checklist of the information you ideally want – other services being used by the customer, their preferences, size of company, or whatever is relevant.

Once you are through to the right person – and this is worth checking, particularly if you have been transferred more than once – you need a structured approach to give you the best chance of success. There are seven key stages to follow (some taking only a few seconds) when making the majority of such calls.

1. A greeting

Greetings should be kept short, simple and to the point. It may be no more than 'Good morning' and can link to check that you have a successful connection: 'Is that John Robertson?'

2. Identification

Any identification should be clear and, allowing for how bad many people are at retaining a name, may contain an element of repetition, 'My name is Forsyth, Patrick Forsyth, from Touchstone Training & Consultancy.' Then, allowing for any response, move promptly on to the next stage.

3. Reason for calling

The reason that you give for calling must be customer oriented, containing a benefit and explaining why you want an *appointment* (do not try to sell the whole product/service at this stage), perhaps mentioning something the customer will be able to see, touch, try out or have demonstrated at the meeting, something which can *only* take place at a meeting.

It helps to speak of the meeting as 'working with the customer' (rather than 'doing something to them'). For instance: 'When we meet we can go through the details together and make sure we come to the right solution' creates a feeling of customer orientation.

4. Request for appointment

There is no substitute for asking for an appointment. However, bear in mind the following:

- Mention the duration of the meeting. Honestly. It's no good pretending you only need 30 minutes if you need an hour. At worst you may arrive and find they have only exactly the 30 minutes you asked for on the telephone.
- Give the customer a reasonable lead-time. They are less likely to refuse an appointment for 7–10 days' time than to refuse an appointment for tomorrow.
- Offer an alternative. 'Would 3.00 pm Thursday afternoon be suitable, or would you prefer a morning, say Wednesday morning?' State the first option more precisely than the second. And use two more and two more if necessary.

5. Respond to objections

Now and again resistance will be met, but you can then employ an objection-handling method called the 'boomerang' technique. This is particularly useful for 'turning' an objection to your advantage. For instance:

Prospect: 'It's not convenient – I haven't the time.'

Sales person: 'It's because I know you're busy that a short meeting may be useful. It will give you the opportunity to hear how we go about things and see whether scheduling more time to discuss the project is worthwhile.'

When you've got them back on track again and sounding even tentatively agreeable, you can 'close' as fast as is polite – with the appointment as your objective.

If it's impossible to make an appointment, you can still achieve something by getting some new information for the records. Having 'won' the conversation and 'negotiation' to that point, prospects will often be in a frame of mind to allow you some concessions and may be quite willing to give you information about future plans, changes or the names of others in the organization you could contact, etc.

Here are four different types of objections you may encounter, with some suggestions on how you can handle them.

The unspoken objection

This is difficult to overcome. It's there, real enough, in the prospect's mind, but is unspoken. Without any feedback other than voice (a puzzled look is not visible over the telephone), you must literally 'read between the lines' to discover when this is happening. If you believe it is then you should ask questions and encourage the prospect to raise whatever is on their mind. This works even to the point of suggesting hesitation: 'I detect a slight hesitation, are you sure Friday is OK? I could equally well do one day next week'; or 'You don't sound sure, I do want to make sure the time is convenient for you; does it really suit?'

The legitimate objection

This is a genuine reason for a prospect's lack of interest. But it may be short-lived, the need may arise later or someone else in the organization might respond positively. If so, the following approaches would be relevant:

Prospect	Sales person
'I'm right in the middle of the budget preparation. I can't see anyone right now.'	'I understand, Mrs Smith. When would be a better time for me to call you back?'
'Thanks for calling, but that kind of decision is outside my authority. It would be a waste of time for us to meet.'	'OK, thanks for that, Mr Black. May I ask who I should contact? Can I say you referred me to them?'

'Look, before you go any further, I can't see us needing your product. We bought something similar a few months ago and, unless there's a remarkable growth in the market, we're fully equipped for the foreseeable future.'

'Ah, I see. Then clearly a meeting now would seem unproductive. I wonder if, rather than us meeting now, you could give me some background information over the phone. ... Thank you very much, Mr Cooper. I'd like to call you again in three months when the growth you spoke about may well have happened.'

Other forms of legitimate objection are a complaint about a minor, but real, product disadvantage; a perceived, but incorrect, product limitation; or a negative past relationship. In all these cases the response should be the same:

- *accept* the prospect's point of view without necessarily agreeing with it;
- *maximize* or correct the point of view by repeating the objection in your own words in the form of a question and playing down its real or perceived impact;
- *compensate* by referring to one or more definite advantages that outweigh the small disadvantage.

The false objection
A false objection is the prospect's argument or excuse for not granting an appointment for a face-to-face interview. As the name applies, it is not the real reason for avoiding a meeting. For example:

'Your product/company just isn't any good.'

He or she is hiding a true objection: what is it that makes the target say this?

'I'm not interested.'

He or she needs more information to become interested.

'Your prices are too high.'

The real meaning here is that the desire for the product is too low.

To overcome these objections you must ask questions and get the prospect to reveal his or her true objection to meeting with you. For example, if – and this is a common one – the point is made that prices are too high, you might say, 'Of course, it is a substantial amount of money, but when you say that, what are you comparing it with?' This focuses the conversation on the real feelings.

'Classic' telephone objections

Prospects frequently state an objection rather than put the phone down on a sales caller. Such objections sometimes have a grain of truth in them but often they are used as part of a game that prospects play to test your resolve and persistence, or your professionalism (are you reading a telescript?) or give the impression that they are less available for an interview than may actually be the case.

The tone of their voice, persistence or conviction will tell you whether an objection is of this nature. The quicker a prospect positively responds to and accepts your reply to an objection, the more likely it is that it will have been this sort. For example:

Prospect	Sales person
'You're just trying to sell me something.'	'No. It's too early to say that! First we must explore your needs and see what sort of benefits from my product you consider important.'
'You'll be wasting your time giving me a sales pitch.'	'That's one thing I won't do. What I would like to do is discuss how we can help increase your productivity and improve your sales. I'm sure our time wouldn't be wasted.'
'Look, just give me a quick description and tell me what it costs.'	'Well, I could do that but I don't believe it would be fair to you. As we offer a wide range of models and prices I can't recommend the right one for you until I understand your

requirements. You could give me a feel for these at a short meeting at which I can show you how easy it is to install any of our models and get their immediate and significant benefits.'

6. Ask questions

While questions are not always necessary, some may be a prerequisite to a good meeting, helping with planning and making sure you are 'on target' once you are face-to-face with your prospect. A checklist of questions that may be necessary in your business will be invaluable.

One hint, which can often be overlooked, is that if you are visiting prospects at their own premises (which they may prefer, particularly for a first meeting) do ask about location. A sentence or two may save you hours of searching. What about parking? Is there a car park?

Similarly, if prospects are visiting your office make sure they know exactly how to find your premises; confirm this in writing (with a map if you have one) and remember to inform others at your office (including the receptionist) as necessary, making sure they know how important the visit is to the firm.

7. Thanks and confirmation

At this stage you should summarize briefly what will now happen: 'Right, I will put that brochure in the post to you, Mr Black and look forward to seeing you, at your office, at 3.00 pm on Monday 27 July.' No more may be required at this stage, though sometimes it's also appropriate to send written confirmation.

Ringing the prospect to make an appointment can be an awkward kind of call to make; you may well be conscious of the degree of 'push' involved, but a systematic approach will make it easier for you to conduct the call and make it acceptable at the other end.

Because of the inherent characteristics of the telephone, those who use it to sell will do better if they bear in mind certain key principles. It is important to look at how you use the telephone itself: your voice and manner; obtaining and using feedback; and planning. The telephone distorts the voice, exaggerating the rate of your speech and heightening the tone. You must talk into the mouthpiece in a clear, normal voice (if you are a woman, it can help to pitch your voice lower). It's surprising how many things can interfere with the simple process of talking directly into the mouthpiece: smoking; eating; turning to write; holding a file or book open at the correct page and holding the phone; allowing others in the room to interrupt; or allowing a bad quality line to disrupt communication (it's better to phone back). These points are all quite obvious, yet it is so easy to get them a little bit wrong and thereby reduce the effectiveness of your communication. It's too late to think of them once you're in the middle of an important call. The paragraphs below review the essentials.

Telephone technique

Voice and manner

Remember that on the phone you only have your voice and manner to rely on in making an impression. None of the other factors of personality is perceptible. Here are some suggestions that may help you to make a good impact:

- *Speak at a slightly slower rate than usual.* Speaking too rapidly makes it easier to be misunderstood and also mistrusted, although, by contrast, speaking too slowly can make the listener impatient or irritated.
- *Smile. Use a warm tone of voice.* Though a smile cannot be seen, it does change the tone of your voice. Make sure you sound pleasant, efficient and, perhaps most important, interested and enthusiastic about the conversation. You will find that enthusiasm is contagious.
- *Get the emphasis right.* Make sure that you emphasize the parts of the communication that are important to the listener, or for clarity. Only your voice can give the emphasis you want.
- *Ensure clarity.* Make sure you are heard, especially with names, numbers, etc. It's easy to confuse S and F, for instance, or find that 15 per cent is taken to mean 50 per cent.
- *Be positive.* Have the courage of your convictions. Don't say 'possibly', 'maybe', 'I think' or 'that could be'. Watch this one; you could give the impression of being circumspect.

■ _Be concise._ Ensure a continuous flow of information, but in short sentences, in a logical sequence and saying one thing at a time. Watch for and avoid the wordiness that creeps in when we need time to think, eg 'at this moment in time' (now), 'along the lines of' (like).

■ _Avoid jargon._ Whether the jargon is that of your own firm (eg abbreviated description of a department name), the industry (eg technical descriptions of processes) or general (eg phrases like 'I'll see to that immediately' – do you mean in five minutes or five hours?), at least check that the other person understands exactly what you mean. They may not want to risk losing face by admitting that you are being too technical for them and a puzzled look will not be visible. Jargon can too easily become a prop to self-confidence.

■ _Be descriptive._ The only pictures people will have in their minds will be those you put there. Anything – such as saying 'It makes programming your video recorder seem straightforward' – that conjures up images in the mind of the listener will prompt additional response from someone restricted to the single stimulus of voice.

■ _Use gestures._ Your style will come across differently depending on your physical position. For example, there may even be certain kinds of call that you can make better standing up rather than sitting down: debt collecting or laying down the law perhaps. Really! Try it; it works.

■ _Get the right tone._ Be friendly without being flippant. Be efficient, courteous, whatever is called for in the circumstances.

■ _Be natural._ Be yourself. Avoid adopting a separate, contrived telephone 'persona'. Consider the impression you want to give: do you want to sound mature, expert or authoritative, for example?

Your intention is to prompt the other person into action. You should speak naturally in a way that is absolutely clear. Here are some useful additional rules:

■ _Be courteous._ Always be courteous.
■ _Be efficient._ Project the right image. And this includes allowing for any equipment you are using: ie, if a computer takes a moment to call up their account number, or if you are typing an address into the system – explain the time it takes.

- *Be personal.* Use 'I' and say what you will do.
- *Be appreciative.* 'Thank you' is a good phrase to use (but don't gush).

Obtaining and using feedback

- *Talk with people, not at them.* As a first step to encouraging a response, form a picture of your listener (or imagine them if you know them) and use this to remove the feeling of talking to a disembodied voice.
- *Remember to listen.* Don't talk all the time. You cannot talk and listen simultaneously.
- *Clarify as you proceed.* Ask questions, checking back as you go along – it may appear impolite to ask later.
- *Take written notes.* Note down anything, everything that might be useful later in the conversation or at subsequent meetings. Get the whole picture and avoid the prospect saying, 'But I said that earlier', which can indicate that your credibility is suffering. And do it as you proceed, not at the end of the call.
- *Maintain a two-way flow.* Don't interrupt, let your prospects finish each point, but make sure, if they are talking at some length, that they know you are listening. Say 'Yes' or 'That's right' to show you are still there.
- *Concentrate.* Shut out all distractions, interruptions and 'noises off'. It may be apparent to your listener if you are not concentrating on him or her alone – it will come across as lack of interest.
- *Don't overreact.* It's easy to jump to conclusions or make assumptions about a person you cannot see – resist this temptation.
- *'Read between the lines.'* Don't just listen to what is said, but also to what is meant. Make sure you catch any nuance and observe every reaction to what you are saying.

KEEPING IN TOUCH

Regular customers need regular contact. What is important here is the total frequency of contact: meetings, letters, notes and the telephone are part of this. But, be careful. Never phone only to keep in touch or, once you have said, 'Hello, how are you?' you may find that you are groping for something to follow it with. Sales people talk of a 'courtesy call'. There is – or should be – *no such thing* as a courtesy call. You need a good reason to call. I don't mean in your terms – that is easy, you want to keep in touch, to remind them of you – but in their terms.

It helps if they expect it. Agree a date: 'I will call you in a month's time' or 'I will be in touch at the end of the quarter.' And a reason: 'To see how the test has gone' or 'To see whether you need more promotional material.' Don't, incidentally, worry about how far ahead such contact is scheduled. If they say to leave three months or six even, so be it. Keep a clear note and get back to them; your efficiency may impress and, from your point of view as long as you have some reminders on a regular basis, it doesn't matter when they originated. Many give up on prospects too soon, just because lead times seem long and then miss business they were in fact half-way to getting.

Think of (and perhaps keep a list of) reasons to call, for example:

- to give them some useful information;
- to update them about something;
- to tell them about a change;
- to feed back something about their operation or service;
- (where appropriate) link to socializing – lunch, dinner, a drink or whatever.

REGULAR ORDER – TAKING CALLS

Real regular 'telephone selling', with dedicated staff who may be full- or part-time, is used in a wide range of businesses, not just classified newspaper/magazine advertising and FMCG (fast moving consumer goods) but also office equipment, plant hire, hospital supplies and many, many more. It's cost-effective. It's not unusual for it to cost £150, even £250 for a person to make a visit, so if the telephone can take one part of the frequency of calling this makes good sense.

The potential benefits

The advantage of this type of activity is that it enables the company to exert much greater control over its sales operations. It can achieve many diverse objectives, far more than just increasing sales. The following are some examples of the kind of objectives that can be set:

- to increase sales to existing customers against budget;
- to liberate sales people's time by reducing routine calling activity;
- to increase the frequency of customer contact;
- to reduce the number of out-of-stock situations in incomplete orders compared to solicited orders;
- to increase the rate at which promotions are sold in;
- to increase the rate of dissemination of information to customers regarding price, uses, packaging changes, brand activity, etc (defined by increases in customer contact);
- to reduce delivery lead time against base period;
- to open new accounts;
- to revive moribund accounts which have not ordered for some months;
- to introduce new lines to customers;
- to negotiate more promotions;
- to merchandise more effectively (defined by a reduction in requisitions for merchandising material);
- to increase average order size;
- to increase the total numbers of orders obtained per week.

As well as the direct effect of the telesales activity, it can free sales people's time, so that more time can be spent on opening new accounts, reviving moribund accounts, selling the full product range, introducing new products, negotiating more promotions, more effective planning, etc.

Will it work for you?

It doesn't work in every circumstance. Telephone selling seems to work best when most of the following criteria are met.

The customers

They must be prepared to accept, or able to be persuaded to accept, coming to the telephone and be accessible by this medium of communication.

They will usually be handling large numbers of competitive products with limitations on storage and cash, so stock levels are an important factor in running their business.

The products

The products must be well known to the customers so that a general awareness can be assumed. If not, telephone conversations will become long and drawn out, with expensive explanations about the product and its performance, frequently ending up with a request by the customer to see the sales person anyway.

The products will normally be of the fast-moving, non-durable consumer type. The average order unit value will usually be quite high.

Ideally, physical stock checks should not be necessary before the placing of an order.

The sales force

The number of actual or potential accounts per sales person will be high.

Calls will be made at regular intervals (while they can vary from once a week to twice a year, accounts with low call frequencies do not respond as well as more active accounts).

The sales force will usually be expected to handle a wide product range and undertake a range of activities.

How to go about it

Telephone selling should not be regarded as a tool that can be used either to replace the sales force or as a cost-cutting means of reducing its size. It works most effectively and efficiently when it is co-ordinated and integrated with existing sales activities. To be successful, therefore, an active telephone selling operation might best be installed in a systematic way, based upon the following steps.

Step 1. Define the objectives

Objectives should be stated in clear, measurable terms, so that the results achieved can be assessed and congruence with the company's marketing objectives ensured. To start such an operation without precise objectives is to predispose it to failure and decay. It's also worth stressing that there are always company politicians who are adept at either recommending that there should be no objectives or at writing opaque, failure-based-ones – consciously, or, worse, unconsciously. Precise targets need to be set for order sizes, conversion rates for telephone calls, number of calls to be made in a set period and so on.

Step 2. Planning and controls

The volume of sales by product and the types of customer to be sold to should be planned; so should the frequency of customer contact. The role of the telephone selling system in relation to the outside sales force should be defined. Existing paperwork and order-processing systems need to be assessed and any necessary changes made so that the telesales operation is compatible with these and communications within the company are able to flow smoothly.

Step 3. Recruitment and selection

The recruitment and selection of competent personnel to operate the telesales function are important and difficult tasks. It's unwise and a false economy to assume that telesales can be undertaken by 'any old spare and under-occupied member of staff'. Telephone selling demands talented and very specialized staff. There are specific skills that must either be possessed or developed by training. There are also basic problems of mental attitude which must be acknowledged if the operation is to be successful. *Note:* such work can be sub-contracted to freelances or agencies. This can work well, though briefing and monitoring are absolutely *vital*.

Step 4. Sell the idea to the sales force

It is essential to sell the idea to the sales people to ensure their active co-operation from the outset. Sales people live in conditions of uncertainty, so are naturally wary and tend to feel insecure when changes are sprung on them. Initially they may be sceptical, particularly because they will have to nominate and submit worthwhile accounts to be phoned. This is important. If sales people are not consulted on this aspect, the operation will start off with built-in competition from your own sales force. Indeed, more than one new operation has faltered in the early stages because sales people were persuading customers not to use the telephone sales service. Sales people should be told why the company is introducing changes, the effect they will have on their jobs and the timetable of actions to be taken.

When recruited, the telephone sales operator(s) should accompany a cross-section of sales people making normal customer calls as part of their training. This will reassure the sales people that these operators are conversant at first hand with the customer, what they look like, what their needs are, what they buy and what they do with the products.

Step 5. Sell the idea to the customers

It is a vital preliminary to achieve customer co-operation and identification with the new system. Customers should be sold the benefits of regular telephone selling, preferably by the sales person on an individual basis.

Step 6. Implement and validate

Like any other marketing or sales tool, telephone selling should be tested on a pilot basis before a company goes 'national' or commits all its resources to it. Its 'testability' over reasonably short periods is one of the factors that make it an attractive technique to experiment with. Initially a controlled implementation should follow the plans drawn up in Step 2. The pilot test should last long enough to provide data on all the variables that could arise, to allow for seasonal fluctuations and to enable a pattern and volume of sales results to be obtained.

This sort of selling can have a positive impact on many aspects of a company's sales operation. However, perhaps it's wise to end this section with a final word of warning to companies contemplating setting up an active telephone sales operation. It must be started for the right reasons – to sell to the right people at the right time and using the right type of trained personnel. There are innumerable stories of companies which thought that all telephone selling consisted of was a desk, a chair, a telephone and any spare, unoccupied member of staff.

A special communication medium

Selling on the telephone is a challenge. It must be done using all the relevant techniques: have a clear objective, make a good start, ask appropriate questions and talk benefits. Objections are just as likely on the telephone as face-to-face, perhaps more so, and must be handled correctly. As with all selling, the aim is to achieve a commitment from the customer, so a firm close is necessary. (You may like to refer back to Chapter 6 for more about these techniques.) But elements are missing on the telephone: we cannot use facial expression for emphasis and complex description is difficult. These and other factors make it a job to be taken seriously. Two things help make it effective.

The first is a moment's thought to ensure the brain is engaged before the mouth. I don't mean a lengthy period of preparation, though certain calls may be well worth planning more formally, but it does mean that the brain must always start working before the mouth opens! Making a few notes and a few moments' thought before dialling are usually well worth while. This kind of planning will help you to:

- overcome tension or nervousness;
- improve your ability to think fast enough;
- prevent side-tracking (or being side-tracked);
- make sure you talk from the listener's point of view;
- assess your own effectiveness.

And, above all, it will help you to set clear and specific objectives designed to gain agreement and commitment from the other person.

Planning is necessary even to cope with incoming calls (at least those that follow a pattern). If you have made plans you will be able to direct or control the conversation without losing flexibility and react to others accurately, without being led on by them. Plan to make difficult calls early and do not put them off – they will not get easier; rather the reverse is true.

To repeat, never think of any call as 'just a phone call'.

The second factor is practice. It's a good idea to know how you sound to a listener at the other end of the line. This is not difficult to organize: a standard cassette recorder or dictating machine on which you can record your own voice is all that's necessary to simulate what you would hear on the telephone. Practise simply by talking and playing back. More usefully, rehearse any particularly important, or often repeated call, which you know you have to make. Better still, get a friend or colleague to hold a conversation with you so that you hear yourself, on playback, responding to questions and conversations that you were not expecting. If you haven't done this before, it's likely that even a few minutes of self-analysis will show you a lot and allow any specific weaknesses or habits to be improved.

Get it right and the telephone is highly cost-effective. What is more, customers get to like it, indeed many telephone sales operators who make regular calls to the same customer every week or month, and then miss one, find the customer is on the phone to the company asking 'Where is my order-taking call?'

Someone like a printer, ordering paper supplies this way, finds it convenient; indeed, if it doesn't work well the printer runs out of paper, and a printer without paper is like a pub with no beer.

Other allied methods

Mobile phones are now ubiquitous, and very useful they are too. The ability to contact customers anywhere, anytime, especially to maintain prompt service, is excellent. Given the frequency with which calls are cut off it may be worth telling customers that you are using one and saying you will call back if there is a problem. There are also still some reservations among customers about calling a number that may be costing them more than a regular call.

Facsimile – *fax* – messages travel by telephone and are worth a separate note. First, I should mention a 'don't'. *Never* send advertisements, or indeed any form of cold canvass, by fax. It ties up the recipient's machine, uses their paper (which costs money) and is profoundly resented; such approaches are self-defeating. This view is not, I think, a personal prejudice. On the other hand, for certain individual approaches and for maintaining contact with current and past customers it can be valuable. It:

- can be less formally worded than a letter;
- has a sense of urgency; and
- rings the changes, adding another method to the sometimes sensitive job of keeping in touch.

Similarly, *e-mail* needs careful use. It can have some of the virtues of fax and be useful for keeping in touch with people you know (and who you know like it), but it is, of course, especially temporary and can be deleted at the touch of a button, so may not be suitable for sales messages that are designed to last.

Neither fax nor e-mail allows a high standard of presentation (as a letter on a smart letterhead does) and this provides another reason for care. The telephone will probably predominate in many kinds of short, sharp sales message for a while longer.

9

Creating Sales Without Leaving Your Desk

The sales office as an agent for increasing sales

I yield to no one in my admiration for the office as a social centre, but it's no place to get any work done.
KATHERINE WHITEHORN

There can be few areas of company activity that contain so ready an opportunity of increasing sales as your sales office. One of the main reasons for this lies in the prevailing standards in business of what now tends to be put under the blanket heading of 'customer care'. Such standards are by no means universally high. Consider: when was the last time you telephoned a company and came off the phone dissatisfied? They took an age to answer, they kept you hanging on, they didn't have the information you wanted or were indifferent, offhand and perhaps even downright rude. All are possible; so is poor follow-up, information not being sent promptly, key information being omitted – you can no doubt recall specific examples, perhaps all too clearly. Yet all these contacts should not only be efficient and caring; they should also be sales-oriented.

In addition, this is a fragile area, in the sense that seemingly minor differences in practice can produce a disproportionate change in the image customers receive – for good or ill – and in the direct effect this can have on sales. A specific example will perhaps make this clear. Awaiting a meeting, I once sat in the reception area of a company producing and selling stationery products and heard the busy switchboard operator (who doubled as the receptionist) repeatedly answering the telephone to customers with the words, 'Are you placing an order or chasing an order?' This brief phrase efficiently enabled her to route the call accurately to the different people who dealt with new orders and with queries. But it did so at the cost of suggesting to *every* caller that orders *needed* to be chased. It's a small point perhaps, but repeated several hundred times a day the company would need to be quite sure it was not diluting the image before accepting it; and such certainty would, I believe, not be forthcoming.

The fact is that such sales office activity cannot be isolated; it appears from the customers' perspective to be bound up with their whole relationship with the company, which makes it still more important. This is well illustrated in the classic training film *Who Killed the Sale?*, which ends with the salesman, who is one of the main characters in the scenario, saying 'I don't know, I just don't know.' Why? Well, in the film, the salesman, working hard to gain an important order, loses it because of a series of mismanaged and seemingly individually minor situations around the company generally and in the area of sales support in particular. The words are his puzzled reply to the question as to why the order was lost.

Consider the background. In most companies, sales do not come from the single isolated success of a sales person calling on a buyer. More often, a chain of events, sometimes occurring over a long period, are what ensure success. This chain of events can begin with the advertising, promotional and other activities that give rise to enquiries. Thereafter, it can involve management, sales people and a variety of others in the company – engineers, estimators and so on, as well as the important (and often underrated) area of 'inside sales'. The mistakes of several of these contribute to the lost sale in the training film.

At its best, this overall cycle of activity is well organized, something the company is aware of and works at matching to the market needs. At its worst, disasters throughout the process can give rise to situations in which orders are lost. Often, as in the film, one person's mistake is not fatal, but the sum total of a number of factors contributes to orders being lost. Sadly, the inside sales staff, sales office personnel, potentially playing a crucial role in ensuring that sales are won not lost, are too often in this sort of position. They are unaware of, perhaps insufficiently briefed about, how their role contributes and are regarded by others in the business as simply administrative 'paper pushers'. A valuable sales tool is then wasted and fails to contribute as much as it could to the company's success.

In the market, it is increasingly difficult for customers to differentiate between competing products. In many industries products are essentially similar in terms of design, performance and specification, at least within a broad price bracket. This is as true of industrial products as of consumer goods. Often, customers' final choices will therefore be influenced by more subjective areas. Customer service can play a major role in this, sometimes becoming the most important factor.

GETTING IT RIGHT

So, how can we get it right and maximize the impact inside sales staff have on sales results? The answer is, primarily, by careful consideration of both staffing and organization.

Running an effective sales office is not easy. The mix of characteristics and considerations that can help make success more likely is not easy to define. It's not enough for whoever manages this aspect of the business to be a _good administrator only,_ though without the sorting out of priorities, without smooth handling of enquiries, files, paperwork, correspondence and records, a sales office will never be effective.

It is not enough for a person to be a _good sales person only,_ though it's essential to have an understanding of and familiarity with sales techniques, and to be able to recognize sales opportunities and ensure they are taken up both by the sales people and members of their team.

It is not enough for the person to an _effective people manager only,_ though it's vital to be able to lead and motivate a close knit and enthusiastic team, tackling a diverse range of activity in hectic conditions; and, in a small company, such people may have a range of other responsibilities.

The manager has also to understand and pass on an understanding of the role of the sales office, so that all concerned see it as a vital tactical weapon in the overall marketing operation. This means that the manager must have an appreciation of what marketing is and of the various ways in which, directly or indirectly, the sales office can contribute to company profitability. This implies acknowledgement of and involvement in this marketing process. For example, if sales office personnel are not told (or do not ask about) the relative profitability of different products, they may be busy pushing product 'A' when product 'B', similar in price or even more expensive, makes more money for the company.

A prerequisite for contributing effectively is for whoever manages this customer interface to be able to *identify priorities*. With such a variety of activities and incoming calls and enquires being so unpredictable, the manager either adheres to a rigid set of rules that allows things to be coped with and runs an adequate office, or has the skill and initiative to recognize different priorities and to get the best out of them, so building up a really effective operation.

Identifying priorities is of little use, however, unless the manager is able to *organize* the sales office to deal with them. This calls for abilities in managing and controlling time, systems and people. To be effective, he or she must be a consistent sales-oriented person manager, able to accept ideas from others and able really to cope with the problems of the *urgent* and balance this with the opportunities of the *important*.

The sales office must be organized to produce an ongoing positive cycle of repeat business from its contacts. Even negative contacts, like complaints, can be dealt with as part of a positive cycle involving a range of possible contacts with the customer, either directly or via other sections of the company. Though possibly low in the company hierarchy, the sales office in fact occupies a central position in the company organization and is vital in terms of contacts and influence.

Next, we will consider two overall areas among those contributing to 'inside sales' being successful.

Success in balancing the administrative/ sales tasks

Most sales offices are characterized by their hectic day-to-day activity. Often understaffed, especially in small companies, sales offices have suffered in recent years from cuts in cost-reduction reviews. While much routine order processing is being automated as part of the 'electronic revolution', a vital part of the role of all sales offices necessitates a personal response. Sales offices deal with a stream of customer enquiries, requests for information and complaints, as well as internal requests from management of all sorts. In no section of the business is the clash between the urgent and the important more apparent.

Constant reviews of administrative tasks, methods and systems are necessary. If administration is under control, priorities can be set for other tasks with specific sales impact and regular work demanded by marked changes taken on, for example:

- the servicing of small orders/accounts;
- making appointments for representatives;
- prospecting for new business; and
- servicing stock replacement orders, etc.

To do this successfully may require close and constructive co-operation with other sections of the company, for example, with production, sales management and the sales force. Poor liaison can cause problems. In one company, for instance, sales office staff spent time handling complaints about delivery on 75 per cent of orders that went through. This was not because delivery was bad (it was reliable and good for the industry), but because (to sound better) sales people were quoting six weeks delivery when everyone in the company knew it was eight weeks. Such unnecessarily wasted time could be used more constructively to increase sales.

Regular changes to routines and systems are now a normal part of commercial life. The saying, 'If your system works well, it's obsolete', contains some truth. Resistance to change and insistence that things must be done the way they have always been done kills the development of efficiency in a sales office and, by allowing administration to become an end in itself, prevents time being spent on more productive sales activity. Even greater acceptance of change will be necessary in future, as the electronic office becomes more of a reality, and it's vital that such change does not dilute the standard of customer service demanded by the market.

Creating sales awareness in all members of the section

Because of the nature of the activity, it is all too easy for staff to see their job as primarily administrative, concerned largely with such matters as:

- providing information;
- answering queries;
- dispatching proposals; and
- sorting out problems (usually caused by others).

But the prime role of the sales office is its role with customers – securing existing business, finding new business and selling on. It has a very direct link with profitability and the success of the company, and response activities must occur in a way that maximizes the chances of making a sale – immediately or in the future.

As mentioned earlier, the prevailing standards of sales office service and selling are not universally high. It should not be difficult, therefore, to make customer contact not only stand out in a way that really impresses customers, but also genuinely increases sales results. For many, this is a real opportunity area.

There are no excuses for not selling. Time pressure, work pressure, staffing, equipment and resources may all make it more difficult, but what ensures real selling does take place is, first, attitude and, second, knowledge and skills of how to do it effectively. Only management can get this over and maintain standards. It's much easier to run a 'tight ship', to set high standards and stick to them, than to let things go by default. People are motivated by belonging to the 'best team' and come to care very much about standards and performance.

Selling must not be confused simply with customer service, however efficient and courteous. This is not to deny the vital importance of service and courteousness, which forms one of the bases for success. Another important basis for success is *product knowledge* – not just knowing about the product but being able to talk about it in a way that makes sense to the customer. This does not just happen. Management must ensure that it does. It's the same with *sales technique*. The sales office team (all of those who have customer contact) must have an appreciation of the sales process, augmented by knowledge of and ability to apply particular skills, on the telephone or in writing, and backed up as necessary by sheer persistence and inventiveness.

Again, this does not just happen. Management is responsible for recruiting the right people, their initial training and ongoing development and for motivating them continuously. It all takes time and the sales office manager has also to plan, organize and control the activity of the office and see they take their own share of the work. It follows that management must concentrate on key issues (good administration and time management helps here), so that they have time for these activities. (*Note:* some of the issues raised in Chapter 6, on personal selling, are as relevant in dealing with people from the office as they are in a face-to-face meeting.)

Having set the scene and illustrated the potential of prompting staff from this area, we will adopt more of a how-to approach and review a number of areas where a sound approach can make a difference. Some of these are simply ideas, while others go into the techniques involved; none – given the right people and sound briefing (perhaps even training) and ongoing management – are expensive, most only demanding a little time and effort. We will start with a brief word on the principal manifestations of customer service which customers expect and react to positively.

CUSTOMER SERVICE

Everyone knows good service when they experience it. At best they say of people who deliver it, 'They are good people to do business with.' But why? What is it that constitutes 'good service'? Normally it must:

- *be promptly available* – customers' patience is very limited and being prompt gives a positive impression;
- *be efficient* – for instance, information must be readily available to avoid delay;

- *be courteous* – there is no situation in which it is permissible to be impolite to customers, whatever the provocation (unless you are prepared for them to cease to be customers);
- *be given in a pleasant, interested manner* – this adds to a good overall impression;
- *look* (or, on the telephone, sound) the part.

And information given must be:

- *specific* – that is, it relates to the exact question asked;
- *understandable* – a clear explanation speaks of care, preparation and concern for the customer, with no confusing jargon;
- *accurate* – the up-to-date information, the exact dimensions, the right figures and so on.

It must also, if it is to be truly cost-effective, be sales-oriented, that is, using all appropriate techniques (see Chapter 6) and with those involved in the sales office being adept at its two main methodologies: the telephone and letter writing.

The telephone

Much of the time in the sales office is spent on the phone, with incoming enquiries and outgoing calls. It is a special medium, and deceptive too. It deserves care and attention and using it well will pay dividends. (This is covered in the section on telephone techniques in Chapter 8.)

But don't wait for calls to come in. In a busy sales office environment, discipline is necessary to keep time available to make outgoing calls. Without getting involved in full-time 'telesales', a great deal of useful ground can be covered. Opportunities to take the initiative include:

- chasing stock orders (where it is agreed that the product will be stocked, where sales will be lost if out-of-stock situations develop even briefly and where regular contact can anticipate and prevent this happening. An example of this might be pen refills in an office supplies provider);
- giving advance warning of a new product or promotion or – more difficult – a price increase (the latter may be linked to a last-chance order at the old price);

▨ giving reminder information (to follow up a neglected mailing, for example).

Also consider arranging to handle small orders/accounts _exclusively_ from the office, without the cost of personal visits by the sales staff. While you may sensibly explain the logic of telephone contact to customers on a first call (in terms of service, _not_ convenience or cost saving to _you!_), once this is accepted such calls can quickly fall into a pattern and provide regular contact orders.

Putting it in writing

Here is a key low cost way of differentiating yourself from others. The prevailing quality of letters sent from sales offices is not high. They tend to be standardized, formalized and, sometimes, less than literate. Even worse, they are introspective, cataloguing things with 'I', 'we' or 'the company', rather than identifying themselves with the customer. As such they can represent a lost opportunity. How does this happen?

Well, walk into any sales office where someone is dictating and listen. Typically, they will look at the information or letter that is prompting a reply and begin: 'A letter to XYZ Ltd, 12 High Road, Marketown – Dear Mr Smith, Many thanks for your letter of 27 January in reply to which I enclose a detailed quotation.' Pause. Only then do they start thinking. But they have already wasted an opportunity by ignoring one of the key rules in writing sales documents – first impressions count.

It may well be the same at the end. The writer (or person dictating) finishes the letter, stops thinking and, with mouth in gear but brain in neutral, adds a final sentence: 'Assuring you of our best attention at all times, we remain, yours sincerely.' Again, this is a waste, adding nothing to the sales power of the text.

Putting together a sales letter along with a quotation, estimate or proposal, is not easy. You need to think about it, sometimes draft it by hand and always follow certain guidelines. Your customers must believe you offer a deal that fully meets their needs in order to buy; not only in terms of the product, but also with regard to price and service.

A proposal or quotation is a tool that helps close a sale successfully. It may not get an order by itself – people sell, not documents – but it can and must help. It has to command attention or it will not be read; it must be understandable or its message will not get across; and above all it must be designed to prompt action.

Before putting 'pen to paper' (or dictating) you need to think clearly about a letter's intentions and ask the following:

- For whom is the message intended? It may not always be only the person to whom it is addressed.
- What are their needs?
- How does our proposition satisfy those needs and what benefits does it give?
- What do we want the prospect to do on receiving the proposal?

You must have clear objectives. Your proposition must be commercially worthwhile; stated in terms of customer needs; realistic and achievable; specific; clear and timed; and capable of evaluation with a yes or no answer.

You must then fit your intentions into a shape that will make sense to the prospect and be persuasive. This format must be well organized, with the flow of information easy to follow, so that the prospect will agree each point progressively. It should also highlight critical areas of particular interest to the prospect, state all the facts the decision-maker needs and summarize all previous agreements. Finally, it should be easily understood by all who may read it and position your organization appropriately.

Either a letter proposal or a formal proposal may be more appropriate in different sales situations. In general, the complexity of the situation and the prospect's methods will guide you in determining which type of proposal to use.

Extra information

In a letter proposal, the critical elements of the recommendations are summarized for the decision-maker. Enclosures, which document your solution or provide extra information, may be added. This approach is most appropriate when a more detailed proposal is not required and recommendations can be clearly presented within the scope of a letter. It is useful when you need only to summarize what has already been agreed, when all the prospect's concerns have been solved or when there is no competition for the order.

A formal proposal is a much more detailed approach, and is appropriate when recommendations are complex or will be perceived as high in cost. When the decision-maker is dependent upon recommenders to make the buying decision, or when no personal meetings have been possible, it's better to send a formal proposal. If you have been unable to meet with all parties, the proposal alone must speak and sell for you. This is a potentially dangerous situation, which you should avoid. No matter how well written, your proposal can never fully substitute for personal sales skills.

Always remember that letters and formal proposals are sales documents. The opening must command attention, gain interest and lead into the main text. First impressions are important – never waste the first sentence. Having gained the reader's attention, the introduction will need to establish background, state the document's purpose and refer to previous agreements.

Exclusive offer

The document should then go on to describe the scope of the prospect's requirements, outline how they will be met and make clear that you understand them. It will suggest solutions, not just in terms of technical details (features), but in terms of advantages and benefits. If possible, the offer should be made exclusive, in that the package of benefits cannot be duplicated by the competition. Reference to timings can also be made at this stage.

Costs need to be stated clearly and related to the benefits of your suggestion and to any intangible factors. It may be useful to amortize costs to illustrate value.

The closing statement will refer to any attachments and should create a sense of urgency so the decision-maker will act promptly. It must close by asking for the order or commitment, making clear what the next action is to be. In a formal proposal, each section may have its own page and a table of contents may help to make it clearer. The letter accompanying the proposal must not be a formality and should add something to the case – perhaps strengthening urgency or specifying further action. The document should be attractively laid out, grammatically correct, well typed, clear and individual – designed for the particular buyer to whom it is addressed.

Layout is more important than trying to squeeze the document on to any particular number of pages. Use headings and paragraphs to ensure clarity. Underlining or a PS may be employed in order to get the required attention. Remember, the intention is to prompt the customer to action rather than demonstrate any great literary skills.

You should try to write as you speak and aim to be clear, courteous and personal.

Things to be avoided include trite openings, pomposity, coldness and clichéd endings such as, 'Trusting we may be favoured with...' Do keep it simple, using short words rather than long ones and one or two words rather than several, particularly clichés or fashionable phrases (eg 'At this moment in time' when you mean 'now').

A final rule: before a document is posted, read it thoroughly. Better still, get someone else to do so as well. It is so easy to read what you want to see rather than what is there. Spell cheques (sic) do not always catch everything. For example, more than one company in the past has lost business to a more careful competitor just by spelling the prospect's name wrongly.

In Chapter 3 the subject of direct mail and effective letter writing was covered in detail. It may be useful to refer back to it in relation to writing sales letters.

BUT...

One other form of contact always seems to find its way to the sales office – complaints. So, at the risk of ending this chapter on a negative note, let's see what can be gained from them in positive sales terms.

Every company gets some complaints – even the best run, with the best products and the best service. Many complaints are minor, but something serious inevitably happens from time to time. How you react and how you deal with complaining customers will determine whether complaints lead to lost customers. You can perhaps think of situations where a well-handled complaint left you more inclined to return to that supplier than if the complaint had never occurred; this is perhaps particularly true of services. Serious complaints usually get lots of action and paradoxically may not lose a customer as quickly as a minor complaint, because minor complaints are often ignored, resulting in a customer who gets *more* dissatisfied as a result of complaining, instead of less.

Considering the amount of time, money and effort that goes into getting new customers, you should obviously take great care to keep the ones you have, and no complaint should ever be thought of as so minor that it can be totally ignored. It is usually up to the sales office staff to handle complaints and it is the sales staff who can take the sting out of complaints and begin to turn a complaining customer into a satisfied customer who is ready to place another order.

Complaints are 'emotive', both for the customer and for the sales staff, and this must be taken into account. In order to make the complaint (something many people actually find difficult) the customer will often get more 'worked up' than is necessary, partly in anticipation of a defensive, argumentative attitude by the company. Your own reaction to criticism is also likely to make you overreact, especially since, in the sales office, you frequently have to answer for the actions of other departments and other individuals. You must take an impartial view, however, remaining loyal to the company and all employees, but above all providing satisfaction for the customer.

Everyone can always learn from mistakes, and you can also learn from complaints. They may, for instance, indicate problem areas within the company, and clearing up that problem area will make things run more smoothly, perhaps improving sales. One particular complaint may bring such a problem area to light for the first time, or it may only become apparent through analysing complaints over a period.

Clearly, you need to look for the meaning behind complaints, as well as trying to satisfy the customer. There must, therefore, be a way of informing management about them, especially when a problem area, rather than one-off mistakes, is indicated.

The best way to do this is through complaint forms, which can be analysed by someone senior in the company and action taken as necessary. It is far better for the system and for morale if this action is seen as being corrective rather than punitive. Complaint forms should not be viewed as black marks for some employee (unless a series of them indicate one employee's poor conduct), but as a system to correct faults. The complaint form is another example of a form which should be tailored to an individual company's require-ments – for more on this see Chapter 10, which looks at systems.

Complaints arise from the following:

- products;
- service functions;
- company policy and conduct;
- employee actions;
- factors outside the company's control.

Whether they are oral or written, there are only two 'types' of complaint: justified and unjustified or mistaken. The information taken from the customer, whether or not a complaint form is used, should be sufficiently detailed to allow its 'type' to be identified. It should provide a basis for prompt investigation, checking and answering of the complaint, either immediately or following investigation.

The paragraphs which follow show how, and the section headed 'Afterwards' looks specifically at ways to 'turn round' a complaint, making it a low cost *sales* contact. The checks and systems should reduce the number of complaints received, but when one does arise it should be regarded as an opportunity, not an embarrassment.

Handling complaints

Complaints should not turn into arguments. They can be emotive and it is all too easy to overreact and become defensive. A systematic approach to any response is useful and helps keep the conversation smooth.

Listen and acknowledge
Listen, listen, listen – it's what customers want. They will not believe you can help until they feel you understand all the circumstances. Say you will listen. Ask them to tell you about it. Say, 'Yes, I understand' and note carefully in writing what is said. This stage also provides valuable thinking time ('How am I going to respond to this?') and needs concentration.

Be sympathetic
Show that you are not going to argue. Never interrupt with 'But...' Apologize, at least for the need for the conversation (you need not admit blame until it is clear that you should).

Clarify
Get the message straight. The angrier someone is, the more necessary this may be. The truth may surface slowly. But avoid casting doubt at this stage; it will make matters worse. Ask and ask again before proceeding with only part of the picture.

Summarize

Repeat the complaint back to them to be sure you have it right, but avoid all emotive language (don't say, 'You claim…'). With agreement on what the problem is, you can proceed to the next stage.

Check

At this point you may need to check, and – if so – beware of delay. Avoid making them hold on too long; offer to ring back, tell them what is happening and how long it will take. Make and honour a promise to get back to them within, or at, a stated time. Give your name if you have not done so already. If this stage is not well handled it will simply sound as if you are being evasive.

The resolution

Then, if a fault is found, provide an answer. If possible accept the blame (*I am* sorry – you speak for the organization) and apologize unreservedly. Make it absolutely clear what action will now be taken to put things right or make up for what has happened and, if necessary, give some concession. In other words, handle it better than they expect. Waive the delivery charge or take action in some special way that they feel is helpful to them and more than is necessary from your point of view. End on a note of thanks ('I'm grateful to you for telling us about this').

Note: sometimes a check uncovers the fact that they are wrong or mistaken. If so, don't rub their noses in it ('It's your fault'). Be diplomatic, save face – blame something else, the urgency, the instruction book or the small print. Try to organize the conversation so that they realize their mistake and tell you what has happened.

Afterwards

While you don't want complaints to occur, when they do and after they have been handled, it's worth looking for opportunities in the situation. Can you make an additional point, create a new contact or do anything to reduce the chances of not being remembered? For instance, follow up with:

- a written apology;
- a reference to the satisfactory outcome at your next contact;

- keeping and using the information the complaint affords (eg did you get a new name at their end or discover anything about the way they work?);
- using the contact to build a more personal relationship for the future.

Don't keep reminding them of the complaint, but keep reminding them of you and your ability to get things sorted and provide good service, even in adverse conditions.

A complaint is still a customer contact and it is contacts on which relationships and businesses are built.

The sales office must not be the Cinderella of the organization, regarded only as being administrative. It is an important part of both service and marketing and, as such, the many contacts it has with customers every day can be a regular way of keeping existing customers and winning over new ones. The cost of handling all of this will be much the same whether it is done well or badly. Poor standards increase costs, not least because any mistakes need more time to sort them out, and – at worst – lost customers need to be replaced. Well done, it provides a low cost way of maximizing business opportunities.

10

Systems to Assist Sales

Systems and administration that work

If your system works well – it's obsolete.
ANON

In Chapter 9 we looked at the impact of the sales office role on service and therefore image and sales. This was stated mainly in terms of the people. Here we review systems. Now for many a small business administration is a distasteful, tedious nightmare; but it has to be done and inefficiencies just make matters worse. If you get behind with the accounts, for instance, you just end up having to pay your accountant more money to straighten things out so that you can report to the tax inspectors without still more time-consuming administration to answer their questions. The principle of running a tight ship and keeping things up to date is clearly sound, even if difficult to practise to perfection.

Whatever overall systems the company may need, the sales systems can and should be kept simple. It is certainly not the intention of this chapter to propagate paperwork, though just a few formats are key. These are reviewed progressively, starting with the first contact with a customer and providing examples from which you can devise a variant which is exactly right for your business. Beware, in fact, of making do with standard forms in this area that do not *quite* work for the detail of your business.

Note: all the forms mentioned can equally well be created on a computer as on paper. Some might even be squeezed on to a smaller handheld device of some sort. (I shall resist naming any, as they change as you watch.)

ENQUIRIES

You need to keep a clear record of every enquiry received. But you need more than this, especially if such documentation is used by more than one person. Your sales enquiry form should act as:

- *a checklist* – a reminder of what to ask, how to handle the enquiry, what details to record and in what order;
- *a prompt* – to further action that may be necessary. Most sales do not come as a result of one action, rather a series is needed, involving telephone, letter, literature and meetings;
- *a record* – this, often thought of as the basic reason, is in fact not as important as the first two, though they all interlock.

The sales enquiry form is a tool to help you sell. Make it earn its keep. Many organizations find it useful:

- to print the form on coloured paper, so that these important documents stand out among other office paperwork;
- to use A4 paper, so that the form fits a standard file and clips easily to any attendant correspondence.

Form 1, shown in Figure 10.1, provides an example. You may want to include space for:

- the time;
- questions;
- account/reference number.

Certainly this format will meet the checklist/prompt/record approach advocated earlier. The bottom half is designed to provide a running

FORM 1 SALES ENQUIRY FORM

TO:	COPIES:
DATE: TIME:	NAME:
ENQUIRY TAKEN BY:	JOB TITLE:
SOURCE:	COMPANY:
	ADDRESS:
SPECIFIC REQUEST:	
	TEL NO: FAX:
	NATURE OF ORGANIZATION
ACTION (I) TAKEN	COMMENTS:
(II) PROMISED	
PROGRESSIVE ACTION PLANNED/TAKEN	
DATE	
COMMENTS ON FINAL OUTCOME:	

Figure 10.1 Sales enquiry form

record, where the last entry is always a prompt to what you have decided should occur next. Thus entries might run:

1/9	Literature sent	(this is the first record)
4/9	Telephone to check whether sales person can follow up	(this is decided on and entered on 1/9)
6/9	Not in for two days. Phone again	(this when the call is made on 4/9)
6/10	Phone – re new budget period	(this when phoned on 6/9 and he says, 'Lets talk about it in a month, when our new budget period starts')

This approach is particularly useful where some time is likely to go by before a conclusion is reached or if the person handling such things is very busy. Don't ever rely on memory and avoid anything that makes you say to the customer, 'Now, where were we on this?' or the equivalent. Customers expect you to know. Even handling 20 or 30 different accounts can allow confusion to arise.

If (when) a successful conclusion comes from an enquiry, the same form may be used to add the following, if appropriate at this stage:

- an order value;
- delivery time;
- account number etc.

If the above is used for what turns out to be a new customer (though it should be completed, in many instances, for existing ones too), then the next job is to create a permanent customer record.

CUSTOMER RECORDS

It is inherently easier to sell more to existing – and satisfied – customers in most businesses than to search for new ones to replace them. So every customer must be carefully recorded.

Form 2, in Figure 10.2, shows a typical customer record card. This may literally be a card, or it may be an A4 sheet or a 'page' on the computer screen.

FORM 2 CUSTOMER/PROSPECT RECORD CARD

	Contact	Position	Ref:	Name:				
1			Type of business:	Address:				
2								
Products used:								
Competitor info:				Telephone____ Fax____				

Date	Call type			Call Summary	Products			Next action
	Cold call	Enquiry	Regular		A	B	C	

Back-up information can be recorded on the reverse side.

Figure 10.2 Customer record card

A variety of information may be useful here beyond the name, address and details of the customer, who they are and what they do:

- personal details (birthday);
- where exactly they are located;
- where you can park if you visit them.

This is often linked to sales records, entries showing what they buy, how much and when (frequency). Together, this information is often referred to as the 'customer database', and is frequently held in computerized form. Database marketing uses such a system to promote different aspects of a product or service range to different customers at different times on an individual basis, and can be used to manipulate the data to match accurately the promotional intention with the type and situation of the customer.

For example, a small accountant might record the financial year of his or her clients. A mailing at the right time might then sell additional services, perhaps extra software for their computer that will make the ensuing annual audit easier or less expensive. Notwithstanding, the simple customer record is always useful and can form the foundation of more sophisticated systems at a later date.

Next, what is needed is something to *develop* business with existing customers.

CUSTOMER DEVELOPMENT

Form 3, shown in Figure 10.3, is a customer development or review form and is primarily a prompt to ongoing action (and is completed progressively, as with the enquiry form, above). Here the basic details go at the top (though this may now simply link to the customer record card) and the planned action is added below.

Three elements different from the customer record are relevant in taking this longer-term view:

1. You may decide not *every* customer needs this form, but in most businesses key ones certainly do. Remember Pareto's Law: 80% of your sales/profits come from 20% of your customers – so 20% may be a good guide to how many should be treated this way.
2. Planned action may include some things beyond the *next* action, for instance:
    – contact at the start of (or before) the financial year;
    – contact when the buyer has completed their first month;
    – contact when the initial order has been in place long enough to produce (positive) feedback.
3. Planned action may be corporate, rather than personal, such as:
    – send tickets for exhibition;
    – send company newsletter with letter;
    – send Christmas card/calendar/gift;
    – invite to event/party.

FORM 3 CUSTOMER DEVELOPMENT FORM

TO:	COPIES:
COMMENTS:	CUSTOMER NAME:
Level of current business:	ACCOUNT NUMBER:
	ADDRESS:
	TEL NO: FAX:
	CONTACT:
	Name Position
Future plans	1
	2
	3
ACCOUNT RESPONSIBILITY:	
ONGOING ACTION	
DATE	

Figure 10.3 Customer development form

Note: as some of these may be planned beyond the next action you need to leave a suitable gap to avoid the form becoming untidy.

One company I worked with referred to what they called the 'LYBUNTS'. When I asked what it stood for, they replied: 'Last year, but unfortunately not this' – they were the lapsed customers, those who had died of neglect. A customer development form is invaluable for making sure this does not happen, and to prompt the individual attention to key customers that can be worth so much. Such information can, of course, be recorded on computer systems so that it can be updated simply. Systems that combine elements such as enquiries, customer information and prompts to continuing action are often called 'trace' systems.

So far so good, but another form is needed in case all is not well.

COMPLAINTS

Any organization, however good, gets some complaints – not too many, all being well, since they should be exceptions. This is only sensible: a 100 per cent quality standard – constantly – is an unrealistic goal, though it is certainly one for which to aim.

Complaints come in all shapes and sizes. They may be caused by lapses in:

- the product itself;
- people, standards of attention, service or courtesy;
- policy;
- a combination of these.

They can also arise from an outside agency, beyond the control of the supplier – a delivery service perhaps.

Complaints must be well handled (see Chapter 9) and, if they are, they can even be turned into positive opportunities to impress customers and encourage them to come back.

But they must also be prevented, and it is here that a system comes in. They must be recorded so that you can learn from experience. Form 4 in Figure 10.4 shows a typical complaints form. Documented and checked, such forms can prevent similar errors causing future complaints, so they must be reviewed regularly.

FORM 4 COMPLAINT RECORD

TO:		COPIES	
DATE:	TIME:		TAKEN BY:
Name:			
Job title:			
Company:			
Address:			
Telephone number:		Fax:	
STATED COMPLAINT:			
ACTION TAKEN:		ACTION PROMISED:	
FOLLOW-UP ACTION (long term)			

Figure 10.4 Complaint record

Sometimes they give early warning of faults that would certainly continue if there were no action on your part; identifying a batch of faulty components perhaps. Sometimes they may identify problems that need a different kind of resolution.

For example, in one company sales people taking orders from retailers were able to arrange for delivery in eight weeks. This happened consistently, reliably and was at least as good as most of their industry and better than some. Customers, however, in what was a seasonal business, sometimes pressed for early delivery. The sales people, eager to please, but knowing the situation could not normally be changed, did not make promises but dropped tangible hints: 'Leave it with me, I don't know what is possible, but I will try for six weeks.' Many customers then rang querying why delivery was not received six weeks later. This was a considerable distraction to the sales office, and in the busiest season too. The fact that a form had to be filled in for every such call and that this was monitored by management, alerted them very quickly to what was happening and allowed action to be taken to stop it. The sales people in this situation were honestly unaware of the disruption they were causing.

A complaints monitoring system and form to match is a sound idea. Now we must look at one more form linked to another potentially difficult area – debtors.

DEBTORS

One of the maxims in business that is totally true is: 'It's not a sale until the money is in the bank.' (So where's my royalty cheque?) So, while this could be considered an administrative matter rather than a sales or marketing one, it is one that sales or marketing should logically take an interest in. Certainly it's one matter that any smaller business has to worry about.

There are three rules: chase, chase and chase again. And a fourth: start as you mean to go on. Payment terms must be made clear at the beginning of a supplier-customer relationship, not left on one side in case they hinder getting the order. Then, as soon as an invoice is overdue, it is chased. Chasing must be systematic, consistent, persistent and aimed at the decision-maker.

Once, a client company asked me to give an opinion on the persuasiveness of their debt-collecting letters – they had eight, sent in sequence and with varying degrees of severity. But, and it was a but which rather invalidated any ongoing demonstration of conviction, each and every one of them was headed, in red, with the words 'Final Demand'! Be aware of the policy at the other end; some companies will never pay anything until it has been chased once (or twice, or…), or unless it quotes the order number – *always* comply with any necessary administration, first time. And have a policy your end. The form acts as a checklist. The letters that you send should be credible and not formulae. Think carefully about who should telephone – which may be the best ultimate chaser – because it can clash with the sales relationship. Remember also that the difficulty with making this kind of call, and it is real one none the less, is psychological. The way debt chasing is done has a bearing on the outcome.

Here is one useful tip. Although it may seem silly, don't reject it without trying it – it works! Stand up when phoning to chase outstanding accounts. If you sit at your desk there is an overpowering temptation to be apologetic and for what you say to be ignored. Stand up and you really will come over more powerfully: 'Now I'm looking at an invoice here that is three months old and we are going to have to do something about it…' You can still be polite; but they will respect the point and, if they get to know you always follow up, they will be more likely to put you on the 'Pay soon' pile rather than on the 'Wait until they chase again' pile.

Finally, we turn to two systems (though they are hardly complex enough to warrant the term) that can help unearth just a few more sales opportunities. These two systems are good examples of taking a creative approach to this area of marketing and can bring large rewards from small inputs.

CUSTOMER OPPORTUNITY ANALYSIS

There are a number of approaches and, while there are more complex ones than those discussed here, the following have the advantage of being simple and costing nothing except a little time.

Rank order

This approach takes a period of time to establish (or some digging into the records) and is really just one way of focusing attention on key accounts (remember Pareto's 80/20 law).

You can use something like Form 5, shown in Figure 10.5, to list customers in rank order, year on year. In some businesses change is faster and you can review quarterly or every six months. A rapid analysis will show where the changes are: which have moved up or down. (*Note:* Form 5 also provides a convenient place to calculate the value of the top 20 accounts.)

Of course, there are positive reasons why a customer may fall to a lower number in the list. Perhaps you know of some temporary reason for the decline in orders: they moved offices, say, and everything was delayed. Or you may have been successful in moving others up the scale, so their order quantity has declined relative to others, not in absolute terms.

The key is to question every downward move. Why has this occurred? Sometimes the reason is internal. For example:

■ the buyer retired and you've not got the name of the new one yet;
■ their geographical position makes them awkward to service and contact frequency has been allowed to drop;
■ a mishandled complaint put the relationship 'on hold' and sharp action is needed to retrieve it.

Whatever the reason, and there may be many, some, when tackled promptly, lead to action which can positively affect sales. It is simple enough and, by reviewing regularly, over time there will always be some to action. For many, the information can come easily off your accounts records, certainly if you use a computer. Used in this way it can prevent large customers suffering any untoward neglect.

Matrix analysis

This approach analyzes sales to individual customers, so again is best developed with your larger ones in mind. Form 6, shown in Figure 10.6, reviews product range alongside buying points.

FORM 5 RANK ORDER ANALYSIS FORM

Customer name	Turnover (T/O)								
	Last year	2 Years ago		3 Years ago		4 Years ago		5 Years ago	
	T/O	T/O	rank	T/O	rank	T/O	rank	T/O	rank
1									
2									
3									
4									
5									
6									
7									
8									
9									
10									
11									
12									
13									
14									
15									
16									
17									
18									
19									
20									
A Total £									
B Total company turnover £									
A/B%									

Figure 10.5 Rank order analysis form

FORM 6 MATRIX ANALYSIS FORM

BUYERS

Client Name:	Training dept/manager	Personnel dept/manager	Marketing dept/manager
Communication Skills Training			
Management Training			
Development of Training Materials			

WORK CATEGORIES (Products)

Figure 10.6 Matrix analysis form

In the example my own firm's range of training services is divided into three (which, I would like to think, is on over-simplification, for it ignores consultancy – and books) and looks at Client X where different jobs have been done for three different functional managers/directors. In a large company this would certainly be possible. Whether work is being done, or perhaps has been in the last year, is shown simply with a tick or cross in the appropriate box. The crosses clearly represent priorities for prospecting.

Such an analysis of larger customers/clients, whose size might lead them to being regarded as good ones in need of no action, can, if carried out systematically, produce a surprising amount of 'new' information and prompt useful sales action which might otherwise not occur.

In more complex situations, and where the figures are available in that particular breakdown (ask yourself if they should be), the actual figures – or even good estimates – can be put in the boxes and a more accurate picture can be shown for review. Many businesses work this way and the product/service range axis can be extended and described as you wish, as can the one listing buyers.

This latter can also represent shops in a chain, a number of branch offices, different geographical locations or divisions, as appropriate.

Again, this is not a time-consuming exercise and can pay dividends, not least in more comprehensive selling across the product range, which can be a perennial problem.

DOTTING THE 'I'S

Finally, it's worth making what may be an obvious point: remember that for the customer what they see is what they expect. In other words, the *quality* of systems has an important effect on image and thus on the likelihood of people doing business with you or doing it again. Consider a hotel: imagine one you like, or at least which aims to make you like it. The décor is good, the atmosphere is pleasant, the facilities are good too – and work efficiently, service is also clearly inherent to their business. Yet, as you leave, the last thing they give you, to remember them by, is the account. Many hotels still seem to give you the fourteenth copy of some obtuse computer printout. It's almost illegible. It's full of alterations and incomprehensible symbols. You need a degree in abbreviations to understand it and, all too often, it contains errors.

You may well be able to think of many other examples. Such action does not inspire confidence in the ability of a firm to deliver, for it is seen as inefficient and uncaring, or both. Have a fresh look at the systems in your office, especially at the systems that show. Are you happy with them all? Do they reflect the image you want and thus actively help you sell? Resolve to review them regularly, as there may be room for improvement and, as we have seen, there is no one image formula to bring in the business you need. Many things contribute, and even systems and administration can play their part. All that may be necessary is to take just a little more trouble than your competitors.

11

The One Hour Marketing Plan

As we saw in Chapter 1, planning is important. The plan for the year may well be an integral part of longer-term planning (say for three years ahead) and the immediate plan must assist.

This one hour marketing plan sets out the basics, the minimum you will need. It will lead you sequentially through the thinking that is necessary for your business to perform. Even an hour's work on this exercise will prove invaluable and trigger ideas.

Your plan will:

- identify opportunities for future profit improvement;
- have the ability to anticipate dynamic external changes;
- provide better protection for the future of the business;
- prompt the collection of relevant data;
- allocate the company's resources towards specific ends;
- allocate those resources with control;
- aim for the improvement of communication around the company;
- provide a proper commercial reference for all activities;
- justify development (and development funds).

If it is to be a practical process, it will help if:

- the approach is both 'bottom up' and 'top down' (ie, it involves people throughout the company);
- the system and purpose are clear to all;
- standard (tailored) formats are used;
- a planning cycle, specifying all timings, is agreed;

- the planning includes a facility to 'fine-tune' (particularly to take advantage of opportunities);
- an eye is kept on the external reactions to everything done to facilitate 'fine-tuning'.

Someone must take responsibility for the planning process (and give some time to it), while others must agree to be involved as necessary. Some discipline may be required here as other pressures too easily intrude. In the context of this book and with smaller businesses in mind, while all aspects of business planning are important, the promotional aspects – the things that will bring in the business – are key.

The process is considered here in two stages. First, we look at the general issues, then at promotion as a key element of the whole.

THE BUSINESS PLAN

Naturally, writing a plan presumes that senior managers know the markets in which they operate, have clear marketing objectives and have the power to authorize or recommend action to agreed cost levels.

All companies should have financial goals expressed in budgets of revenue and expenditure (see Form 1 in Figure 11.1) and the first task is to note them.

However, since sales and profits can only be made from customers in the markets we select, the first task must be to translate the financial objectives into market objectives. They must answer the question: 'What results must be achieved in the market place to produce the financial objective we wish to see?'

Meaningful answers can only be produced by considering two interrelated analyses:

1. What opportunities and threats will be present?
2. What are the strengths and weaknesses of the company?

These together form what is called a SWOT analysis (Strengths Weaknesses: Opportunities Threats). This only means taking a hard, objective look inside the company and at the market, before setting down more of the plan. Using Forms 2 and 3, in Figures 11.2 and

FORM 1 FINANCIAL GOALS

Financial Objectives		
Revenue (by product)	Last year's actual	Next year's plan
A		
B		
C		
D		
Total		
Costs		
Profit		
Comments:		

Figure 11.1 Financial goals

FORM 2 STRENGTHS AND WEAKNESSES

Company

Strengths   Weaknesses

Action:

Figure 11.2 Strengths and weaknesses of the company

11.3, you can make notes of the strengths and weaknesses of the company, and the opportunities and threats in the market, along with action to be taken.

Here are the kinds of questions that should be asked.

Internal strengths and weaknesses

What is our customer base?

- Who do we deal with (by size, location, industry, etc)?
- What is the customer mix (eg which category is most important)?
- Are our customer groups increasing/decreasing in size?
- How dependent are we on our largest customer?

Range of products/services

- Does it accurately reflect market needs?
- How does it compare with competitors?
- Is it too narrow/too broad?

Prices/price policy

- How do we set price?
- Are we competitive?
- Are we seen as offering 'value for money'?

Promotion and selling

- Whom do we communicate with, how often, in what way?
- What do they know/feel about us?
- Are we selling the range?
- Are sales contacts seen as providing good service?

Internal factors

- Does our planning help the business?
- Is individual responsibility well defined?
- Do we set appropriate standards/targets and measure and control to fine-tune performance?

FORM 3 OPPORTUNITIES AND THREATS

Market

Opportunities   Threats

Action:

Figure 11.3 Opportunities and threats in the market

Market opportunities and threats

What do we know about our market?

- How large is it (how many potential customers)?
- What do they currently buy?
- How much do they buy (eg annual/monthly spend)?
- How often do they buy (ie frequency)?
- Who do they buy from?
- How do they find/locate potential suppliers?

What do customers think of the market?

- Why do they buy?
- Why do they buy the way they do?
- What do they think of the product/service (eg good value, over-priced)?
- What do they think of the service from suppliers?

How is the market served competitively?

- Who are our direct/indirect competitors?
- What are their strengths/weaknesses?

What are the trends?

- Is the market growing, contracting, changing, restructuring and how is the competition reacting?

Gathering good information can, for example, provide you with insights into how and why people buy, which may in turn prompt the development of sales approaches that are better than the competition and therefore provide an opportunity (which links to an internal strength). Conversely, the development plans of a competitor may represent a threat.

There is more here than can reliably be kept in mind, and thinking it through and making some notes that may influence action is valuable.

The next step is to translate financial goals into marketing objectives that bear in mind the SWOT analysis, then, with the objectives in mind, to identify strategies that could be pursued. Form 4, in Figure 11.4, relates to objectives and strategies.

The difference here is crucial:

■   the *objective* is a desired result in the market place;
■   the *strategy* is a course of action to achieve that result.

Let's take these in turn. Without objectives, it is impossible to focus and to place any tactical activities in order of priority. Yet, the main options available to us in marketing objectives are limited, perhaps to six:

1. *To increase market share.* In a static market this can be done by 'conquest selling' or winning business from competitors.
2. *To expand existing markets.* This objective will focus on selling the fullest range of products/services to existing customers and markets. It also presumes very close co-operation between those who are involved in different aspects of the business.
3. *To develop new products/services for existing markets.* This marketing objective can involve simply the revision of existing products/services, or the introduction of the radically new.
4. *To develop new markets for existing products/services.* This is more attractive and lower risk than some options, but is finite, especially so in some service areas where demand is already being met.
5. *To develop new products/services in new markets.* This is an example of true diversification. This usually carries the highest risk of all marketing objectives. Many companies do not even consider such objectives. Future pressures, however, for the growth necessary to keep good staff, may force a reassessment.
6. *To improve the profitability of existing operations.* When growth opportunities are limited, many companies must in the short term seek higher returns from higher productivity and greater cost-effectiveness of their operations.

From the analysis of market opportunities and threats and the internal assessment of strengths and weaknesses, we can select the marketing objective(s) that will best achieve the financial goals for the planning period.

Next, objectives must be linked to strategies, the purpose of the strategy being to focus effort, coordinate action and exploit the

FORM 4 OBJECTIVES AND STRATEGIES

Strategies:

Figure 11.4 Objectives and strategies

identified strengths of the firm. By corollary, the purpose is also to avoid wasting resources on peripheral and non-productive activities.

Clearly, different objectives will require very different strategies. For instance, the two might line up like this:

Marketing objectives	Some possible strategy alternatives
To increase share of the existing market	Marketing segmentation and concentration of resources on selected segments. Developing product/service applications and range extension. Range of registered firm names for different segments
To expand existing markets	Increasing the frequency of customer purchase. Increasing product/service usage (in other applications). Opening new branches
To develop new markets for existing products/ services	Expanding the range of segments currently dealt with. Overseas expansion
To develop new products/services in new markets	Diversification by purchase/take-over. Technological extension. Exploitation of corporate resources and skills
To increase profitability of existing business	Improving the total product/service package offered to each account. Marketing audit and productivity analysis. Reduction of product/service range

The selection of strategies need not be mutually exclusive. Often a combination can provide an even stronger effect in marketing plans. However, the greatest danger at the point of selecting appropriate strategies is that we may be tempted to adopt too many courses of action. Such a mistake spreads management too thinly and prevents commitment of maximum effort to the prime and most important courses of action.

Marketing planning, then, must begin with a thorough and creative attempt to choose the most appropriate focus of the entire firm's marketing effort. The determination to concentrate simplifies the tactical marketing plans which must then follow for the range of products/services to be offered, the prices to be charged and the promotional and selling actions to communicate with the chosen markets.

Next, using Form 5 (see Figure 11.5) we turn to products/ services and price. There are factors to be considered here, such as product lifecycle and positioning, which are beyond the scope of this book; however, we do need something that will prompt ongoing thinking about both. Products need to be changed, updated and must keep up with the market; services too. And price must be watched constantly for profitability and competitiveness; such decisions must not become merely formulae. A small firm, without long decision-making processes, may be able to steal an edge of competition with their use of price. I once saw an independent petrol station compete very successfully on price with a large group rival across the road because it took them two minutes to decide what price to set, whereas their larger rival took two weeks to liaise with head office before a change could be made.

With products/services, you need to consider particularly that:

- long-established, mature products/services may remain the same in principle as they were years ago, but they will have to change in detail to meet changing customer needs;
- new products/services may have to be developed, both to meet new customer needs and to keep out competitors who see them as a means of ultimately acquiring more business;
- there may well be opportunities to offer a range of differently priced variants for different customers and different situations;
- as a harsh economic climate forces corporate customers to seek productivity improvements in all functions of the business, so they become more demanding, but the same pressures may also produce new opportunities.

With prices, ask yourself these questions:

- How aware are customers of price – the actual levels and the hourly rates (eg car servicing)?
- How do customers perceive price? Does, for example, a higher price imply in their minds higher quality, or do they view price as a commodity factor with no differentiation between firms?
- Are there 'price barriers' in a customer's mind which must be avoided in any quotation for business (eg £100 or £10,000)?
- How far can we price differentially because of the perceived and accepted reputation we have?

FORM 5 PRODUCTS/SERVICES AND PRICES

Unchanged products	
Modifications to existing products	
Products	Action/timing
New products	
Products	Action/timing
Deleted products	
Products	Action
Price	
Products	Action

Figure 11.5 Products/services and prices

Price is a critical area of the marketing mix and one that tends to receive too little analytical attention. Far too often the decision is simply to keep in line with the competition or to work essentially on a cost-plus basis. In fact, price should reflect the overall policy at the strategic level and show creative flexibility at the tactical level, up or down, depending on the threat or opportunity.

THE PROMOTIONAL PLAN

Successful promotional activity needs to be based on a continuous process of review and action, and preparing and implementing a comprehensive promotional strategy demands time, skill and a systematic approach.

The checklist below makes clear 12 key points which will then be examined in more detail. They can be considered under five main sequential stage headings: analyzing the company's needs; preparing the operation plan; pre-implementation preparation; implementation; and the post-analysis of results.

Promotion plan checklist

1. Analyze the market and clearly identify the exact need.
2. Ensure the need is real and not imaginary and that support is necessary.
3. Establish that the tactics you intend adopting are likely to be the most cost-effective.
4. Define clear and precise objectives.
5. Analyse the tactics available, taking into consideration the key factors regarding:
   - the market;
   - the target audience;
   - the products/services offered;
   - the firm's organization/resources.
6. Select the mix of tactics to use.
7. Check your budget to ensure funds are available.
8. Prepare a written operation plan.

9. Discuss and agree the operation plan with all concerned and obtain management approval to proceed.
10. Communicate the details of the campaign to those involved in implementing it and ensure that they fully understand what they must do and when.
11. Implement the campaign, ensuring continuous feedback of necessary information for monitoring performance.
12. Analyze the results, showing exactly what has happened, what factors affected the results (if any) and how much it cost.

Analyze the company's needs

The prime difficulty in the analytical stage is not so much the identification of the need, but ensuring that the need is real and not _imaginary_.

Identification of a need can come from:

- formal research;
- own company investigation;
- professional staff;
- specific market demands; and
- our own observations.

Such analysis is part of the total marketing review (and SWOT). Promotionally we are primarily concerned to show clearly the inter-relationship of customer categories (ie the kind of firm/organization/individual they are), products/services and business (ie new business – a new client, extension – an existing customer buying more, etc). We may well have to plan different strategies to impact specific areas, for example to produce sales to a particular kind of business with whom we have not had prior contact.

Once a need has been clearly identified, it must be established that the kind of support you intend using is likely to be the most cost-effective method of fulfilling that need. Then the planning stage can commence.

Preparing the operation plan

The first stage of any plan must be the quantification of the objectives. A clear statement of exactly what you want to achieve, put as specifically as possible, is needed. 'To improve business' is just not precise enough, whereas an objective which states, 'To improve the number of new customers buying Product A by 50 per cent this year' makes it clear to everyone exactly what needs to be done and above all how success will be measured.

Once the objective is finalized the selection of tactics can take place. This will depend on a number of factors, including the following.

The market available

- What is its nature?
- Is it buoyant or is it in a low period?
- Is it price-sensitive? If so, how?
- What is the competition doing?
- What is the customer profile?

The target audience

- Types of people/organization?
- What are their buying habits?
- What motivates buyers?
- What are their current attitudes to promotion?

The products/services we offer

- What is our current performance?
- What are the strengths and weaknesses?
- What promotional support has it received in the past?
- What capacity is available?
- What is its market profile/image?
- What is its position in the life cycle (ie is it seen as new and interesting or old and dull)?

Organization of the firm

- What are our current sales and promotional methods?
- Would some tactics cause internal difficulties, eg in terms of administration or resources?
- Is the company involved in any other activity that might affect what we want to do, or detract from it?

Having answered these questions, there may still be a number of alternative tactics, all of which could be suitable for achieving the objective. Which tactic to use will depend on which is the most cost-effective.

Once the decision on tactics has been made, the details should be formalized into a written operation plan. It is always worth writing this down, even in a small firm. This should not be a one-off exercise, but will eventually provide a reference, which can be updated regularly so that it always sets out the plan for the next period. Planning of this nature is a 'rolling' process. It should include:

- background information as to why the promotional support is necessary;
- the objectives;
- profile of the target audience(s);
- reference to product/service details;
- details of additional support other than that which you are actually planning, perhaps that being done by associated offices, or various staff;
- budget details – how much the action is estimated to cost;
- details showing exactly how the plan will be implemented;
- controls, standards and methods of obtaining results;
- an action plan, or timetable, showing what actions are required, when they should be carried out and by whom.

There are a variety of ways of making the decision on the budget more logical, for example using comparisons with competitors, standard percentages of revenue and so on. (This concept was developed in Chapter 1.)

Pre-implementation preparation

As long as the operation plan has been correctly prepared, the pre-implementation preparation should be a formality.

This can only be achieved if the operation plan has been discussed and agreed with everyone concerned with the support activity, well before any action is required. This can ensure you pick up ideas (or identify snags) from everyone in the firm, some of whom may surprise you with their constructive comments.

Don't forget, either, that if everybody feels involved they will more readily commit themselves to the next stage.

Implementation

The success or failure of any promotional activity, provided it has been thoroughly planned, rests on how well it is implemented. The effectiveness of the implementation will depend on how well the details are communicated around the company and then controlled. Therefore, the details of what is to be done must be communicated in such a way that they are clearly understood by everyone.

Effective methods of controlling the implementation must be set up to obtain maximum feedback while promotional activity is running. This will permit any necessary changes to be made at the earliest opportunity.

The post-analysis of results

Any promotional campaign can involve a great deal of personnel time and is often expensive in terms of opportunity cost. This is true regardless of what is spent on the other aspects.

You therefore want to know how money is being spent and what achievements are obtained from that expenditure. Examining the detailed results of every form of promotional activity will show clearly:

- what the situation was prior to the activity;
- what we aimed to achieve (the objective);
- what the situation is after the promotional activity has ended (and what we have achieved);

- whether there are any factors outside our control which might have influenced the result, what they were (eg competitive activity, legislation changes) and their effect;
- what has happened to the rest of the market or at least our near competitors;
- what the effect might have been had we not carried out the promotion;
- what the budget was and how it was spent.

Careful analysis of what has been achieved is important, not least as part of the planning and consideration of what to do next, which should be occurring in a continuing cycle.

No promotional activity plan can be carried out in isolation, particularly without linked sales follow-up and service along the way. This must be planned too, so, as an addendum to Form 6 (see Figure 11.6) – the promotion plan, Form 7 (see Figure 11.7) focuses on sales.

Here we should think about and list who will do what:

- How much prospecting will be done; when, how, by whom?
- Who will follow up leads, to what time-scale?
- What sales targets are necessary?
- What record will be kept?

Planning and implementing a soundly based systematic promotional plan is not easy, nor is ensuring that all the back-up resources, people, skills and systems are geared to converting the initial enthusiasm created in potential customers into actual business. But it is certainly necessary and, done successfully, it provides a sound basis for securing and, more importantly, enlarging your business.

Note: most people plan and work with the promotional plan (Form 6) best if it is in the form of a calendar. This creates an ideal rolling plan (a perpetual year planner will give you a 12-month view at all times) and the detail will fill out as time goes by. Thus, in January, 99 per cent of the activity will be listed for, say, January to March, whereas only half may be able to be listed at that point for the next part of the year. Using a wall chart, with plenty of space, tailoring the headings to your business will provide a practical planning and implementation tool and also show, at a glance, the relationship in time terms between different activities.

Finally, it may be worth having one last sheet, Form 8 (see Figure 11.8) on which to note 'other issues'.

FORM 6 PROMOTION PLAN

	Advertising	Promotion	Public Relations
January			
February			
March			
April			
May			
June			
July			
August			
September			
October			
November			
December			

Figure 11.6 The promotion plan

FORM 7 SALES PLAN

Sales plan

Individual targets

Name	Target

Actions/timing

Name	Action	Timing

Figure 11.7 The sales plan

FORM 8 OTHER ISSUES

Issues		
Action	**By whom**	**By when**

Figure 11.8 'Other issues' – implications for the rest of the business

This flags the implications of the rest of the plan for other elements of the business. Here are some examples:

- Does a sales initiative (involving formal presentations perhaps) necessitate training being done in advance?
- Does recruitment need to build in the new skills required in future?
- Does the organization or structure need changing (eg a new job description)?
- Do systems/controls need adjustment?

Business planning, and its marketing components, is a broad issue. The foregoing represents a minimum approach; it should not put you off doing more (and investigating more) but think carefully before omitting the thoughts or actions implied in any of the areas that are specified. A sound foundation makes everything in this book more likely to hold up.

Afterword

An afterword allows an author to have a last word and make final comments on the basis that readers have read all or most of what has gone before. So, what are the key issues here? Of course, every business may discover that some things are more important than others. Maybe you find that mail shots are a key part of your promotion or that some edge you have created in providing a particular level of service is what makes the difference. But there is likely to be one common factor.

Bringing in the business is not a simple matter. There is no magic formula and it does not just happen. Without a doubt success goes, at least in part, to those who best manage the process. It needs thinking through, it needs clear decision making about options and priorities and, perhaps above all, it needs coordinating. The prizes go to those who are prepared to do the planning and be persistent.

This is not, of course, to dismiss other matters. You need a good product or service. You must conduct the business in a way that provides good service. Many other factors, from setting the price to collecting the debts, will have a bearing on the matter. Once such things are set, promotion – the whole process of bringing in the business – must become a continuous part of the activity. It cannot be put off, or saved for those moments when you have time (this may in fact be just the wrong moment to be doing it and besides you will never have enough time), but must become a permanent part of managing the business.

Thinking this way involves deploying the techniques reviewed and discussed in the previous pages; it is also a habit. Those who develop the habit of ensuring that their business is 'promotion-led' will tend to do better than those who simply hope something will turn up.

As you put this book aside resolve, if nothing else, to work in a way that acquires this habit. Doing so is likely to bring better returns and, in the long term, will take less time and cost less.

The business success you have in the future is always related to the action you have taken previously. What you do makes a difference.

References

BOOKS

Birn, R (1999) *The Effective Use of Market Research*, 3rd edn, Kogan Page, London

CBD, *Current British Directories*, CBD Ltd, London

Direct Mail Databook, Gower, Aldershot

Forsyth, P (1996) *101 Ways to Increase Your Sales*, Kogan Page, London

Forsyth, P (1997) *30 Minutes Before a Presentation*, Kogan Page, London

Forsyth, P (1997) *How to Be Better at Writing Reports and Proposals*, Kogan Page, London

Forsyth, P (1999) *Everything You Need to Know About Marketing*, 3rd edn, Kogan Page, London

Forsyth, P (1999) *Marketing Professional Services*, 2nd edn, Kogan Page, London

MIA, *Meeting with Confidence*, MIA Ltd

Royal Mail, *Go Direct*, Royal Mail

VIDEOS

I Wasn't Prepared for That, Video Arts Ltd, London

Who Killed the Sale?, FT Management, London

Index

Administration   5, 189
Advertising   15, 24, 35
Advertising media   37, 42
Appointments   133, 168

Benefits   122
Bonusing   89
Brochures   15, 57
Budgets, promotional   17
Business cards   27, 109
Business names   28
Business plan   217
Buying process   118

Cold calling   114
Competition   4
Complaint form   209
Complaints, handling   196,
      208
Cooperative advertising   90
Copy 'hooks'   72
Copywriting   44
Creativity   58, 69, 90
Customer care   185
Customer development   132,
      206
Customer needs   7, 123
Customer record system   204
Customer service   131, 191
Customers   7, 125

Database marketing   206
Debtors   210
Demonstration *see* product
      demonstration
Direct mail   15, 49
Directories   117
Display material   90

E-commerce   12
E-mail   184
Envelopes   56
Events   54, 136
Events, planning   139
Events, venue   144
Exhibitions   100

Fax   183
Features   123

House style   15

Image   15
Incentive schemes   90
In-home promotion   87
In-store promotion   88
Internet   115

Jargon   107, 128, 175

Language   53, 154
Letterheads   28

Letters   58, 77
Lists *see* mailing lists

Mailing lists   52, 116
Mail shot   55
Market approaches   11
Market research   8, 42
Market Research Society   11
Marketing concept   2
Marketing definitions   2
Marketing function   2
Marketing plan   216
Mobile phone   183

Name badges   28
Need identification   129
Networking   117

Objections, handling   170
Organization   231
Overseas markets   12

Pareto's Law   206
Persistence   133
Planning   5, 21, 121, 139
Post Office   56
Presentations skills   135
Press publicity   15
Press relations   28
Press release   30
Pricing   226
Prizes   96
Product demonstration   157
Product knowledge   120, 122

Products   6
Promotion budget   17
Promotion mix   14
Prospecting   114, 165
Prospects   52
Public relations   15, 24, 27

Questioning techniques   129, 173

Reply devices   66
Reply, paid   67
Response rate   67

Sales letters   193
Sales office   131, 185
Sales promotion   15, 86
Sales techniques   118
Selling   15, 112
Services   6, 120
Sponsorship   48, 93
Strategy   223
SWOT analysis   217
Systems   201

Telephone selling   164
   set up   179
Telephone techniques   174, 192
Trade advertising   43
Trade promotion   89

Web sites   39, 50, 81

Yellow Pages   37, 114, 116